CONFLICT

CONFLICT

Journeys through war and terror in Southeast Asia

Nelson Rand

Every effort has been made to contact the copyright holders of material reproduced in this book. In cases where these efforts have been unsuccessful, the copyright holders are asked to contact the publishers directly.

PUBLISHED IN 2009 BY MAVERICK HOUSE PUBLISHERS.

Maverick House, Office 19, Dunboyne Business Park, Dunboyne, Co. Meath, Ireland.
Maverick House Asia, Level 43, United Centre, 323 Silom Road, Bangrak, Bangkok 10500, Thailand.

info@maverickhouse.com
http://www.maverickhouse.com

ISBN: 978-1-905379-54-5

Copyright for text © 2009 Nelson Rand.
Copyright for all pictures Nelson Rand.
Typesetting, editing, layout, design © Maverick House.

5 4 3 2 1

The paper used in this book comes from wood pulp of managed forests. For every tree felled, at least one tree is planted, thereby renewing natural resources.

The moral rights of the author have been asserted.

A CIP catalogue record for this book is available from the British Library.

To Tyrants and Oppressors:
Lest we forget what threatens your sound sleep.

CONTENTS

ACKNOWLEDGEMENTS

The idea for this book began in March 2007 from a meeting I had in Bangkok with Jean Harrington, the managing director at Maverick House Publishers. Many thanks go to Jean for her advice, encouragement and support, without which this book may have never been written.

During the writing process, several people provided me with valuable feedback, input, and editorial advice, for which I am very grateful. Many thanks go to George McLeod, Ross Milosevic, Oliver Talbot, Russ Iger, Paul Murray, Robert Petit and Matt Wheeler.

Countless other people deserve thanks, many of whose names I don't even know. From guides who smuggled me into forbidden areas, to people who let me document their suffering, to soldiers who watched my back in battle: thank you for sharing your world— and at times your nightmares—and thank you for showing me the resilience of the human spirit.

PREFACE

Driven by youthful ambition and an addiction for adventure, in January 1998 I travelled to the northwest Cambodian town of Samrong in search of war. Just north of the town, government forces were battling Khmer Rouge guerrillas and troops loyal to the recently deposed first prime minister, Prince Norodom Ranariddh, who was ousted the previous July in a coup by his co-prime minister, Hun Sen.

Immediately upon arriving in Samrong on motorbike from the tourist town of Siem Reap, I met a Japanese war photographer named Toru Yokota who would give me my first and only lesson in combat photography. We ordered some food at an outdoor restaurant and he began to brief me on the current situation when we were interrupted by the sound of an incoming mortar. Instinctively, I hit the ground for cover, and by the time I looked back up, all I could see was Toru grabbing his camera bag and running as fast as he could towards the explosion. While the mortar landed off in the distance, Toru's lesson had a direct impact: in combat photography, as in life, the reward lies not in turning away from the fire, but in going towards it.

This book spans a decade, beginning in Cambodia in 1998 during the final months of the country's long and torturous civil war. Government forces had just taken over the last Khmer Rouge stronghold of Anlong Veng when I arrived at the town during late April with the aim of launching my career as a journalist. Drawing mainly on my two trips to Anlong Veng in April and June 1998, chapter one focuses on the collapse of one of the most brutal revolutionary movements the world has ever known.

In August 2000 I moved to the Thai town of Mae Sot on the Thai-Burmese border in order to document a little known war between ethnic guerrillas of the Karen National Liberation Army (KNLA) and one of the world's most repressive military regimes. Over the next three years, I made several trips into Karen State with the KNLA, accompanying them into battle on numerous occasions and witnessing the endless struggle of Karen civilians trying to survive the onslaught of brutality being waged against them by Burmese government forces. This is the subject of chapter two.

In April 2004, after much planning and organizing, I visited a remote group of Hmong guerrillas and their family members in northern Laos who had been holding out against Lao government forces since 1975. In one of the most tragic legacies of the Vietnam War, about 15,000 Hmong soldiers who fought in a CIA-backed secret army in the 1960s and 70s fled to the jungles with their family members after the communist takeover of the country in 1975. Some are still living there, desperately struggling to survive as government forces continue to hunt them down. Like the Hmong, many of Vietnam's Montagnards also fought alongside US forces during the Vietnam War, only to later be betrayed and forgotten. About 10,000 Montagnard soldiers fled into the jungle in 1975 with promises of US support and fought on for another 17 years. While no longer engaged in an armed struggle, Vietnam's Montagnards continue to be repressed and persecuted by their government. Between 2001 and 2003 I made several trips to Vietnam's Central Highlands and to Cambodia in order to document the plight of the Montagnards, including those who had recently fled Vietnam to seek sanctuary in Cambodia. The tragic betrayal and abandonment of the Hmong of Laos and of Vietnam's Montagnards—two of America's most loyal wartime allies ever—is the subject of chapter three.

The final chapter of this book is set in southern Thailand where government security forces are battling an Islamic insurgency. This chapter is mainly set in March 2008 when I spent a month in the area, including a week in which I was embedded with a company of the Thai army.

While this book draws heavily on my personal experiences, the aim is not to tell my story, but the story of these conflicts and of the people caught up in them. It is by no means a general book about war in Southeast Asia (for there are many conflicts that I haven't covered here), but rather, it is a book about the particular conflicts of Southeast Asia that I have journeyed through.

Nelson Rand,
Bangkok, April 2009.

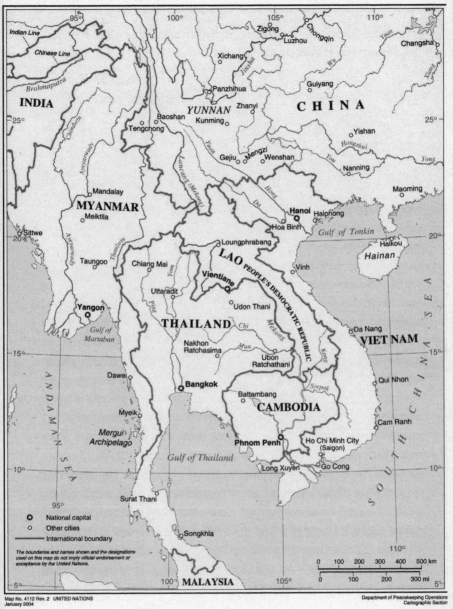

CHAPTER 1

CAMBODIA:

THE DEATH OF THE KHMER ROUGE

CAMBODIA

THAILAND

LAO PEOPLE'S DEMOCRATIC REPUBLIC

Samrong

Cheom Ksan

Siempang

BANTEAY MEANCHEY

Poipet

SIEM REAP

Phnom Thbeng Meanchey

STUNG TRENG

RATANAKIRI

Boung Long

Sisophon

PREAH VIHEAR

Stung Treng

Lumphat

Angkor Wat

Siem Reap

Battambang

BATTAMBANG

KAMPONG THOM

KRATIE

MONDOL KIRI

Pailin

Tonle Sap

Kampong Thom

Senmonorom

Moung Roessei

Pursat

Kratie

PURSAT

Kampong Chhnang

KAMPONG CHHNANG

KAMPONG CHAM

Snoul

VIET NAM

Kampong Cham

GULF OF THAILAND

Krong Koh Kong

KAMPONG SPEU

Phnom Penh

Prey Veng

PREY VENG

KOH KONG

Kampong Speu

Ta Khmau KANDAL

Benam

SVAY RIENG

Sre Ambel

Takeo

Svay Rieng

Chhak Kampong Saom

KAMPOT

TAKEO

Sihanoukville

Bok Kou

Kampot

SIHANOUKVILLE

CAMBODIA

◎	National capital
◉	Provincial capital
○	Town, village
✈	Major airport
	International boundary
	Provincial boundary
	Road
	Railroad

The boundaries and names shown and the designations used on this map do not imply official endorsement or acceptance by the United Nations.

0   10   20   30   40 mi
0   20   40   60 km

CAMBODIA

It was April 1998 and one of the most brutal revolutionary movements the world has ever known was on the verge of collapse. Mass defections and a concerted military offensive by the Royal Cambodian Armed Forces were threatening to do to the Khmer Rouge what the radical movement had done to Cambodia: destroy it.

Pol Pot, the tyrannical despot who had led the communist group until he was ousted in June 1997, was dead by the middle of the month. All that was left of his movement was a dwindling band of committed insurgents holed up in the rugged mountains straddling the Thai-Cambodian border, just north of the town of Anlong Veng.

Since the early 1980s, Anlong Veng and its surrounding area had been a Khmer Rouge enclave and one of its main guerrilla bases from which it tried to retake Cambodia and launch a second revolution. Few outsiders had ever made it to Anlong Veng, and of those who did, several never returned. While some journalists had made it to the town since July 1997, it was still shrouded in mystery that April as government forces were battling to take control. It was both a town under fire and a town undergoing change; history was unfolding in the flames of war. It was a town I had to get to, and a fire I had to see.

I arrived in Cambodia about a week after Pol Pot's death on 15 April 1998, with the aim of traveling to Anlong Veng to launch my career as a journalist. This wasn't my first trip to Cambodia or my first time to the frontlines of its civil war. I had been living in Vietnam for much of the past year, studying Vietnamese and navigating my way through a doomed relationship, and often visited Cambodia—lured by its danger, excitement, political instability and, ultimately, by its war.

Cambodia pulled me, while Vietnam pushed me away. So when I finished my final exams at Vietnam National University in Ho Chi Minh City, completing my classroom studies for an undergraduate degree in Asian Studies, I said goodbye to my girlfriend and traveled across the border and into Cambodia.

My first stop before facing the fire in Anlong Veng was the northwestern town of Siem Reap, the gateway to the famous temples of Angkor. In the 13th century, the Kingdom of Angkor was one of the most powerful in Southeast Asia with its territory stretching far into what is now Malaysia, Thailand, Burma, Laos and southern Vietnam. It is the grandeur of this past kingdom that Cambodia has tried, unsuccessfully, for over 500 years to rediscover since it was invaded and sacked by the Thais in 1431 AD. Few kingdoms in the history of human civilization have had such an impact on the national consciousness of a country. Being both a blessing and a burden for Cambodia, it serves as a perpetual reminder to its people of what they are capable of achieving; but ironically, it also reminds them of their failure as a nation to actually attain such glory again.

In the 1980s, most of the area around Siem Reap was controlled by the Khmer Rouge, which used its temples as shelters and shields during their war against the Vietnamese, who toppled them from power in January 1979. This ended Pol Pot's reign of terror and forced his communist movement to retreat into the jungles, regroup and transform itself back into the guerrilla army that it was before it came to power in 1975.

By 1998, however, Siem Reap was firmly under Cambodian government control and quickly becoming one of the most popular tourist destinations in Southeast Asia. Traveling there was easy, but getting to Anlong Veng, situated 120 kilometers farther north, was another matter. The road from Siem Reap to Anlong Veng ended after about 60 kilometers, turning into a jungle track at a place called O'Bai Tap, which was sheltering thousands of people who had fled the recent fighting and turmoil in Anlong Veng. Surrounded by malarial infested jungle and landmines, Anlong Veng was virtually cut off from the rest of Cambodia, which was precisely why the Khmer Rouge was able to hold onto it for so long. I knew in order to get there, I had to first get to the refugee camp at O'Bai Tap.

Without much of a problem I negotiated a ride with the driver of a motor-taxi who was more accustomed to taking tourists to temples than journalists to refugee camps, but he didn't seem to mind the long-distance fare, at least that is what I thought.

Setting out in the early morning, we made our way north on a quiet road that meandered its way through the tranquil Cambodian countryside, passing through ancient Angkor. With its long abandoned temples half-hidden in the jungle, neglected and scarred from years of civil war, the gentle yet battered landscape seemed a reflection of Cambodia's soul. Passing through it was a calming prelude to the fear and uncertainty that I knew lay ahead.

The refugee camp at O'Bai Tap was still nowhere in sight when the road prematurely turned into a jungle cart-track, making my driver reluctant to take me any farther. I urged him to continue on, reminding him that our deal was for him to take me to O'Bai Tap, not to some forest track. After riding on for several more minutes, he suddenly stopped and ordered me off his bike. As soon as I dismounted, he pointed an imaginary gun to my head, pulled its trigger, and then drove off in the direction from which we came. I was left stranded alone in the forest, and stunned at his violent charade.

I didn't know whether his gesture was malicious or intended as a caution. Nonetheless I decided not to turn back. Instead, I cursed and resisted my fear, and continued on foot, not knowing how far I'd have to walk to make it to O'Bai Tap, if I was walking in the right direction, or even if the trail I was walking on was landmined. Sometimes it's best not to think at all.

Before I had time to change my mind, a Toyota Land Cruiser pulled up behind me, slowly navigating the jungle terrain. Excited, I flagged it down. The driver was a Caucasian man in a military uniform.

'Who are you?' he asked, obviously surprised to see a lone foreigner on the jungle trail.

'I'm a Canadian freelance journalist trying to get to Anlong Veng,' I replied, hoping it didn't matter who I was.

'And who are you?' I asked back, surprised to see a white man in military dress driving a jeep through the jungle.

He introduced himself as the United Nations Defense Attaché and he was heading to O'Bai Tap to investigate the latest developments of the conflict. He agreed to give me a lift to the camp and he later told me he also wanted to get to Anlong Veng, but believed he might not be able to make it.

'I think it's impossible,' he said. I disagreed, but kept my opinions to myself. As far as I was concerned, if the Cambodian government had a presence in Anlong Veng, then it would be possible for me to get there as well. The only thing I needed to do was find an army unit in O'Bai Tap that was on its way to the front and I could tag along with them, similar to four months before in Samrong when I hopped on an army truck transporting troops to the frontlines at O'Smach on the Thai-Cambodian border.

Unlike Anlong Veng, however, O'Smach was not a Khmer Rouge stronghold and was relatively accessible, albeit dangerous because of the fighting. At the time, it was being used as a base for royalist troops loyal to Prince Norodom Ranariddh, who was ousted by his co-prime minister, Hun Sen, in a coup on 6 July 1997. Troops loyal to Ranariddh's FUNCINPEC party withdrew from the capital following the coup, fleeing to the country's northwest, and digging in at O'Smach on the Thai-Cambodian border. By April 1998, however, fighting had eased at O'Smach and a shaky ceasefire was in place, leaving the main front of Cambodia's civil war at Anlong Veng.

We arrived at the refugee camp at O'Bai Tap shortly after I was picked up in the forest. The camp was situated on a barren piece of land, where approximately 4,000 people lived in shelters made from bamboo and plastic tarpaulin.

These people had escaped from Anlong Veng, having fled the recent fighting and the Khmer Rouge. For many, it was the first time they had been outside of Khmer Rouge territory for years, even decades.

They left an area where poverty was encouraged and private enterprise was treacherous. Self-initiative was discouraged and trading outside of Khmer Rouge territory was illegal. Months before, the Khmer Rouge had issued an edict which banned the use of tin to build houses in Anlong Veng, because tin was deemed to be for rich people. At about the same time, smoking was banned, the only music allowed was the Khmer Rouge theme song of the revolution, and women were forbidden to wear makeup.

Ta Mok, a one-legged military commander who had ousted Pol Pot from power and took control of Anlong Veng and the Khmer Rouge in June 1997, wanted to keep his people poor and angry so they would fight the government more resolutely.

But his plan backfired. Instead of firing up the population to fight, he encouraged them to flee, to defect to the government, and even fight against his forces.

Disgruntled by Mok's repressive policies, economic hardship, and from fighting a never-ending war, a secret, eight-member 'break-away committee' was formed in Anlong Veng some time in late 1997 or early 1998. It consisted of officers from Khmer Rouge Division 980, based south and southwest of Anlong Veng town, and was led by Yim Phanna, the division's commander. In late January, Phanna met his cousin, a Siem Reap woman who periodically crossed into Khmer Rouge territory to visit her rebel relative, and told her about his plan to breakaway from Mok. A couple of weeks later, after government officials learned of Phanna's plan, the Siem Reap woman went from being a vegetable seller to a secret government agent when the deputy chief of intelligence of the Cambodian army offered her a mission: hand carry letters into Khmer Rouge territory and deliver them to Phanna. She agreed. After making two separate trips in late February and early March 1998, a meeting was arranged between five of Phanna's delegates and government officials at the residence of the deputy governor of Siem Reap province. A deal was struck: the committee would lead the break away but would wait until the end of March so that government forces could be in place to liberate Anlong Veng.

But before the breakaway began, Mok was informed of the plot. On the night of 22 March, he fled Anlong Veng into the escarpment of the Dangrek Mountains, about fifteen kilometers north of the town. He collected most of the Khmer Rouge's political leadership, including Pol Pot (who was under house arrest), the group's mobile radio transmitter and, along with a few hundred loyal troops, launched counterattacks against the plotters who were now backed by the Royal Cambodian Armed Forces. As fighting broke out, several thousand civilians and soldiers fled south to O'Bai Tap, while over 30,000 fled north into Thailand. By 4 April of that same year, nearly 2,000 Khmer Rouge guerrillas had defected to the Cambodian government.

While O'Bai Tap held a wealth of information about life under the Khmer Rouge, my inexperience as a journalist combined with my determination to make it to Anlong Veng prevented me from capitalizing on the opportunity to interview those who could have given me first hand accounts of life under the Khmer Rouge. For me, the story was in Anlong Veng, not in O'Bai Tap, so I busied myself with trying to find a lift to the frontlines rather than documenting the stories of those in the refugee camp. Unfortunately, I couldn't even do that. When the defense attaché was going back to Siem Reap and I still hadn't found a lift to Anlong Veng, I took the easy way out and accepted a lift to Siem Reap.

I arrived back in Siem Reap that night, feeling ashamed of myself for giving up so easily. Why didn't

I stay the night in O'Bai Tap and wait for a ride the next day? Why didn't I just start walking? Why did I succumb to my fear? I looked inside myself that night and didn't like what I saw. It scared me. In fact, it scared me straight back to O'Bai Tap the following morning.

Armed with my shame and newfound determination, I arrived back at the refugee camp with no intention of repeating the failure of the day before. Since there was no Land Cruiser offering a comfortable return journey to Siem Reap, and no one saying it's impossible to get to Anlong Veng, things were looking up. I immediately approached a group of government soldiers, offered them some cigarettes and inquired about getting to the front. I was in luck. They were on a re-supply mission that was leaving for Anlong Veng later that day and were more than happy to give me a lift. Shortly afterwards, we set out for the grueling journey in an old Russian truck, leaving O'Bai Tap and my shame behind.

The journey took about six hours. The road was nothing more than a track that wound its way through the thick, inhospitable jungle that had been a successful buffer zone between the Khmer Rouge and government-held territory for years. While Anlong Veng was overrun by government forces in 1994, it was recaptured in less than a month as it proved too costly for the government to hold, mainly due to the difficulty of transporting troops and supplies to such an isolated region of the country. Navigating the trail in an old Russian truck was no easy task, and certainly this obstacle would have been carefully considered by any military planner. On several occasions we broke down or got stuck, making the journey painfully slow.

The sun was just beginning to fade into the grayness of dusk as we approached Anlong Veng. On arrival, we made our way to the town's center, passing deserted bamboo huts, felled trees that were waiting to be logged and exported to Thailand, empty farmhouses, and the town's picturesque lake lined with coconut and mango trees. With the exception of government soldiers camping in the town, it was virtually empty; a ghost town haunted by more than just ghosts. There were rumors of mass graves, of bodies submerged in the lake, of skeletons in the fields. This was a town where evil had resided; the postal code of mass killers. Few communities could have claimed a higher proportion of mass murderers within its population, or such widespread fear among its citizens. To be a good member of the Anlong Veng community required absolute loyalty and servitude to the masters of the town.

Among the masters were Pol Pot, Brother Number One until he had his long-time defense minister killed (along with his wife and 13 of his family members and aids) in June 1997; Ta Mok, the Khmer Rouge's army chief and the defacto governor of Anlong Veng, who was also known as 'the butcher'; Khieu Samphan, the Khmer Rouge's leading intellectual who almost starved a nation to death when a PhD he wrote on his desire for an agrarian society was enforced as government policy during the Khmer Rouge's reign of terror; and Noun Chea, a despot who tricked his half-paralyzed cousin out of his home in 1975 with promises of a revolutionary reward and then had him executed. These were just a few of Anlong Veng's more accomplished leaders. Through the windshield of the Russian truck, Anlong Veng spread out before my eyes, the last Khmer Rouge enclave and the stronghold of my fear.

After we entered the town, we pulled up at a large building, most likely the town's communal hall, which was now operating as a command post for the Royal Cambodian Armed Forces (RCAF). When I climbed out of the truck, an ageing commander, probably in his 60s, greeted me with a welcoming smile and offered me a hammock and a space in the hall to spend the night. He recalled some French from his childhood and he spoke to me in the language of Cambodia's former colonial master before he invited me to share a can of tuna for dinner.

Other soldiers were able to speak some Vietnamese, which enabled us to communicate, and a couple of soldiers could speak some English as well, so I soon found myself among newfound friends. In good company but exhausted from the day's journey, I retired to my hammock early and fell asleep to the sound of distant mortar fire.

The main frontline was about ten kilometers north of the town. I awoke early in the morning and set out to reach it. I began on foot, but before long I was picked up by a tank unit heading to the front, whose smiling soldiers seemed just as thrilled as I was to be riding on the back of their tank.

With the last remnants of the Khmer Rouge pinned down, outnumbered and out-armed, the RCAF soldiers I was with certainly had something to smile about. They were on the verge of defeating the movement that had terrorized their country for decades, and now they were about to end Cambodia's long and torturous civil war. But there was no victory parade just yet. There were still several hundred, if not more than a thousand, hardcore guerrillas and several diehard commanders holed up in the nearby Dangrek Mountains, which straddled the Thai border. With mass murder on their hands, these commanders weren't about to give up without a fight—and certainly death would not come easy for a movement that thrived on it. Prepared for battle we pushed on, passing a destroyed tank before setting up position to launch an artillery assault into the mountains.

As the tank crew prepared for the attack, zeroing the gun barrel on the enemy target and chain-sawing a nearby tree that was in the line of fire, I chatted with some soldiers and snapped a few pictures before positioning myself beside the tank, ready to photograph the artillery assault. The tank was in the middle of the road while I was just in front of it to the right, hoping to capture an artillery round as it came out of the barrel, remembering an impressive photo taken by Toru near O'Smach that depicted the same thing.

After an anxious wait, the commander finally gave the order to launch the attack.

'Three ... two ... one ... fire!'

The earth-shattering blast almost knocked me to my knees, leaving me dazed and questioning the result of the picture I had just taken. I recomposed myself and tried again from the same position for the second launch.

'Three ... two ... one ... fire!'

Again the blast shook me, and again I doubted the quality of the picture taken. For the third round, I opted for a different position, to get a wide-angle shot which captured more of the scenery. I decided to do this just as the commander began his countdown to fire, so I sprinted off the road to try and get into position.

'Three ... two ... one ... STOP!'

The commander aborted the launch at the last second and screamed at me not to move. I looked over my shoulder and saw the soldiers on the road frantically waving their arms and yelling a single word over and over, 'Mines!'

In my effort to get the picture, I had run into a minefield.

I froze. My world came to a standstill producing a single frame of dread. All my thoughts and energy focused on the moment and what I needed to do to survive. I looked down at my feet, cautious not to move, then I looked back to the road, carefully calculating what to do. The road was only a few meters away, but it was a distance no gauge could measure in terms of fear.

With a rush of adrenaline, I pivoted on my right foot and lunged back with my left, gently placing it down in the imprint of my previous step. I quickly repeated the motion with my right foot, and then with my left, trying to minimize the surface of the ground in which I stepped and never putting both feet down at the same time.

Carefully, step by step, I made my way back to the road, where the soldiers of the tank unit cheered me on, gunning for my safe return before they resumed their attack. I'd like to say I plotted the course perfectly, but I think I just guessed it and got lucky. I reached the road in a state of euphoria, high on a cocktail of adrenaline and relief, but before I had much time to bask in my victory, the attack continued.

'Three … two … one … fire!'

I stayed on the road and settled for a close-up picture, indifferent as to whether it would turn out or not. I really didn't care about the previous pictures either.

I spent that night with the tank unit camped out in an abandoned village near the frontline. During the evening, an RCAF soldier proudly showed me, among his meager possessions, a collection of photographs that he carried. They were mostly of him, his family, and several women, but one picture in particular caught my interest. It was a picture of an elderly man holding a small child. The man was smartly dressed in casual clothes, standing barefoot in a wooden house and holding the child in his arms like a loving father.

Behind him there was a wooden rocking chair, a pair of slippers and the faint image of a girl sitting on the top step of a staircase. What stood out most in the picture, however, was the man's warm and gentle smile, a smile that radiated from his face as he posed for the camera. A date imprinted in the bottom left hand corner of the photograph read 86/4/6 (presumably, 6 April 1986).

The man in the picture was Pol Pot, and I assumed that the child he was holding was his daughter (however I later learned that his only daughter was born in 1986 so unless the date was incorrectly set on the camera, it couldn't be her for the child looks to be at least 12 months old). The soldier told me he had found the picture in a deserted Anlong Veng house. Knowing that pictures of Pol Pot were extremely rare, I realized I was looking at an historic and potentially valuable photograph, especially since it showed the architect of Cambodia's killing fields in a completely different light: as a loving, caring man. The picture gripped me. Here was one of history's most prolific killers, Cambodia's harvester of death, nurturing a small child, something that he took from countless of Cambodians. The irony struck me right away, but it was his smile that really struck me. He was portrayed as such a nice man, not a sadistic tyrant who murdered one fifth of the Cambodian population. Intrigued at the picture, I offered the man five dollars for it. He was the happiest soldier in the village.

I found it difficult to sleep that night, not because of my newly acquired picture, but because of the incoming mortars being fired by the Khmer Rouge. The guerrillas had at least two pieces of artillery on the escarpment, and judging by the number of rounds they were firing throughout the night, they were making good use of them. While the mortars were landing far enough away from our sleeping quarters so as not to injure us, they were landing close enough to scare us awake throughout the night. The soldier sleeping next to me was getting irritated, and after one such explosion he grumbled, 'The Khmer Rouge never sleep.'

Indeed, for all the brutality and ruthlessness associated with the Khmer Rouge, that soldier's complaint summed up one thing that is often overlooked about the movement: that it was an effective guerrilla army. In seven years from 1968 to 1975, the Khmer Rouge grew from an underground movement that defended its headquarters with bows and arrows and a handful of guns to a governing authority that assumed complete control of the state. It came to power two weeks before the North Vietnamese took over South Vietnam, making it the first and fastest communist victor in Southeast Asia. After it was routed from power by the Vietnamese in January 1979, the Khmer Rouge spear-headed the Cambodian resistance and slowly wore down the world's fourth largest army for a decade. In April 1998, the guerrilla group wasn't collapsing because of its ineffectiveness on the battlefield, but because of its ineffectiveness off of it.

The Khmer Rouge, formally called the Communist Party of Kampuchea, came to power on 17 April

1975. On that day the radical movement turned from a predominantly guerrilla group to the ruling party of the state. It rose to power through a seven-year insurgency and a brutal civil war that left Cambodia shattered. Its rise to power also occurred in the face of massive US bombing campaigns between 1969 and 1973, which ironically played a major role in increasing support for the Khmer Rouge among the rural peasantry. These bombing raids targeted Vietnamese communist bases and supply routes in Cambodia, but the colossal civilian death toll and devastation caused by the bombings ultimately drove tens of thousands of peasants into the welcoming arms of the rural-based Khmer Rouge.

The guerrillas also received an upsurge in support among the rural peasantry after the country's leader, Prince Norodom Sihanouk, was ousted in a coup in 1970. The coup brought to power a right-wing pro-US regime led by General Lon Nol and prompted the exiled prince to form an alliance with the Khmer Rouge. Sihanouk became the nominal head of a Khmer Rouge-dominated government-in-exile backed by Beijing and appealed to Cambodians to launch a campaign of guerrilla attacks and civil disobedience against the government of Lon Nol. Sihanouk's popular support in the countryside extended the Khmer Rouge's influence and many peasants joined the insurgency in the belief that they were fighting for the restoration of the monarchy, which Lon Nol had abolished. Before long, the ranks of the Khmer Rouge had swelled to over 100,000 soldiers and followers, most of them rural peasants ignorant of any political ideology.

With support from China and North Vietnam, the Khmer Rouge made rapid gains against the US-backed Cambodian army. Despite receiving over $155 million in American assistance, Lon Nol's poorly trained and unmotivated forces were no match for the zealous revolutionary fighters of the Khmer Rouge and its experienced, well-equipped allies of the North Vietnamese army and Viet Cong, who used Cambodia as a staging ground for the liberation of South Vietnam. By the beginning of 1971, three years after the Khmer Rouge had launched its insurgency with just a few thousand followers, it controlled over half the country's territory. By the end of 1974, General Lon Nol's forces controlled little more than the capital of Phnom Penh, the city the Khmer Rouge called 'the great prostitute on the Mekong'.

The revolution was led by a charismatic school-teacher-turned revolutionary named Saloth Sar, the man who became known to the rest of the world as Pol Pot. The Khmer Rouge emerged from the devastation of rural Cambodia to start a revolution that would damage the country even more. When its forces captured and marched through Phnom Penh in April 1975, they were greeted with cheers of joy, having successfully overthrown the corrupt, incompetent regime of Lon Nol and bringing to an end their devastating war. But few would be cheering by nightfall.

The Khmer Rouge's ineffectiveness off the battle-field was reflected in their very first political act, on the very day they came to power. They ordered the immediate evacuation of Phnom Penh, forcing its two million inhabitants to leave for the countryside at gunpoint. Thousands perished along the way. The Khmer Rouge's goal was to turn the country into an agrarian, classless utopia, and the evacuation of Phnom Penh was the first step towards achieving this. In what would become one of the most radical social experiments in human history, every Cambodian city and town was emptied; money, markets and private property were abolished, schools were closed, hospitals were shut, religion was banned, family ties were split, officials of the previous regime were executed, and the country was turned into a vast slave labor camp. Pol Pot also erased more than 2,000 years of Cambodian history when he declared Year Zero that month; the country's borders were sealed, foreign embassies were expelled, and Cambodia all but vanished off the map. In the following three years, eight months and 20 days in power, an estimated 1.7 million people died as the Khmer Rouge tried to create this unattainable utopia.

As part of its revolution, the Khmer Rouge wanted to regain territory that had historically belonged to the Khmers. Priority was given to Vietnam's southern Mekong Delta region, known in Cambodia as Kampuchea Krom (Lower Cambodia), which was gradually taken over by the Vietnamese in the 17th and 18th centuries and officially ceded to Vietnam by the French in 1949. The Khmer Rouge wasted no time in trying to take back Kampuchea Krom and began launching military campaigns into Vietnamese territory within days of coming to power. Naval forces attacked several Vietnamese islands in the Gulf of

Thailand during the confusing, final days of the civil war in Vietnam, and then launched a cross-border land attack the day after South Vietnam fell to the communist North on 30 April 1975. War-ravaged Vietnam couldn't even enjoy one day of peace before its new war began with the Khmer Rouge.

While relations warmed temporarily after more than a month of sporadic fighting, brazen cross border attacks by the Khmer Rouge resumed in 1977. On 30 April of that year, as Hanoi celebrated the second anniversary of its liberation of South Vietnam, Khmer Rouge forces advanced ten kilometers into Vietnam, slaughtering hundreds of local inhabitants and razing schools, pagodas and entire villages. In September, a similar campaign was launched in which Khmer Rouge forces advanced 15 kilometers across the border. Such raids were bold and brutal and aimed to 'annihilate the Vietnamese on their own territory'. Annihilation meant murder, rape, torture, mutilation, decapitation, disembowelment and many other forms of human misery. In the September 1977 attack, many of the several hundred victims were found with their heads cut off, eyes carved out, stomachs ripped open, or limbs chopped off. In a raid in April 1978 on the Vietnamese village of Ba Chuc, all but two of its 3,157 inhabitants were killed in an orgy of violence that saw women raped and left to die with stakes planted in their genitals.

While Vietnam was the main focus of the Khmer Rouge's irredentist dreams and foreign aggression, Thailand and Laos were also targeted by Pol Pot in military campaigns throughout his reign. At the same time the Khmer Rouge was provoking its eastern neighbor in 1977, it was also launching raids into Thai territory and aiding the Communist Party of Thailand. Pol Pot was pursuing a brazen foreign policy that few leaders had ever done in history: militarily provoke all of its neighbors at the same time.

At the heart of the Khmer Rouge's confrontational policy towards its neighbors was the irrational belief that its forces were far superior to them. This was exemplified in a radio broadcast in May 1978 when the Khmer Rouge announced it could defeat its powerful Vietnamese enemy because one Cambodian soldier was equal to 30 Vietnamese. Using this irrational calculation, the Khmer Rouge believed that if one fourth of Cambodia's eight million people took up arms, they would be able to defeat the Vietnamese because two million Cambodian soldiers could kill 60 million Vietnamese and the enemy's population was only 50 million. Such irrational thinking, which coincided with paranoia, produced a lethal dose of self-induced destruction.

Throughout his reign, Pol Pot was obsessed with the existence of internal and external enemies of the Communist Party of Kampuchea and the revolution it was launching. While Vietnam was viewed as the main external enemy, internal enemies were not so conspicuous. In a meeting of high-ranking party members in December 1976, Pol Pot warned that there were 'evil microbes' buried inside the party that must be located and exterminated. The result was a never-ending purge of party members that ultimately corroded the Khmer Rouge from the inside out. As one such purged party member told his torturer at the notorious S-21 interrogation center in Phnom Penh, 'If you arrest everyone, there won't be anyone left to carry out the revolution.'

At S-21, thousands of purged party members and officials were tortured into making false, elaborate confessions such as working for the CIA, KGB and the Vietnamese—all at the same time. Such a fantastic plot, which senior Khmer Rouge leaders genuinely believed, was nothing short of delusional. And the more people they purged, the more paranoid they became. Any person a prisoner named under torture would also be suspected of being an enemy, so the more people who were purged, the larger the number of people were incriminated, and the more people who were incriminated, the more paranoid they became. It was a vicious circle. Thousands of loyal party members died because of Pol Pot's paranoia, which in turn weakened the party and its grip on power.

Today, S-21, or Toul Sleng as it is commonly called, is a museum complete with thousands of mugshot photographs of the victims, instruments of torture, and human skulls. It is now one of Phnom Penh's most popular tourist sites and serves as a grim reminder of the horrors of the regime. What few visitors realize, however, is that the majority of the 'victims' at Toul Sleng were senior Khmer Rouge officials who were purged of their ranks, innocent of the crimes for which they were accused—innocent of being traitors to the Khmer Rouge cause. The real victims, of course, were the women and children (mostly wives and children of senior officials taken to S-21, although many of the women were purged Khmer Rouge officials as well), while the heroes were the unknown number of S-21 prisoners who were actually guilty—for guilty at S-21 meant treachery to tyranny.

As a final paranoia-driven death blow, Pol Pot made a sweeping purge of the country's strategic Eastern Zone (the zone bordering Vietnam) in the spring of 1978, just as all-out war with the Vietnamese became imminent. Convinced that the zone was flooded with people that had 'Khmer bodies but Vietnamese minds,' Pol Pot had thousands of cadres, officials and soldiers making up the military and civil administration of the zone killed. The zone secretary, So Phim, took his own life before he was arrested. Over a quarter of a million people were deported to other areas of the country and probably 100,000 more perished in the single bloodiest episode of Pol Pot's rule. The purge was fatal: it severely weakened the Khmer Rouge's capacity to wage war and defend against the Vietnamese. While the Khmer Rouge viewed Vietnam as its number one enemy, the more ruthless of the two was the Khmer Rouge itself.

On Christmas Day, 1978, the Vietnamese launched a full-scale invasion of Cambodia in response to the Khmer Rouge's repeated attacks and incursions into its territory. Over 100,000 soldiers in six motorized columns swept across the border backed by air support from captured American-made aircraft, while an amphibious force invaded along the coastline. Vietnamese forces captured Phnom Penh and overthrew Pol Pot's regime in 14 days, shattering the Khmer Rouge's theory that one Cambodian soldier was equal to 30 Vietnamese. In 14 days, the Khmer Rouge went from being the ruling party of Democratic Kampuchea—the official name of the Khmer Rouge regime—back to what it was best at being: a guerrilla group.

The typical historical canon of the Khmer Rouge ends in January 1979, with the Vietnamese invasion and defeat of the regime. But the next phase of the Khmer Rouge story is equally fascinating as the group received a bizarre rebirth and became one of the greatest benefactors of the Cold War.

In order to escape the invasion, which was viewed by the West as an expansionist communist endeavor by the Vietnamese, the top Khmer Rouge leadership fled to the Thai-Cambodian border along with several thousand troops. Despite the regime's collapse, its leadership remained intact. Its army, although shattered, was not completely destroyed. The Khmer Rouge may have been on its death-bed, but it wasn't dead.

The presence of Vietnamese infantrymen on the Cambodian-Thai border greatly worried Thailand, a key ally of the West, while Beijing was infuriated that its Khmer Rouge ally was ousted by China's historic enemy, Vietnam, which was supported by China's Cold War rival, the Soviet Union. The recipe was ripe for a Cold War showdown in Cambodia, and the murderous Khmer Rouge took center stage.

Only five days after the fall of Phnom Penh, the Khmer Rouge's foreign minister, Ieng Sary, met the

Chinese leader Deng Xiaoping in Beijing. Sary was promised Chinese support for fighting the Vietnamese and offered an immediate US$5 million. A fund was soon established at the Chinese embassy in Bangkok in which senior Khmer Rouge officials could withdraw up to $5 million at a time, with an annual limit of $80 million.

Thailand, for its part, agreed to give sanctuary to the Khmer Rouge and even allowed shipments of Chinese arms and ammunition to pass through its territory. In return for Thailand's support to the Khmer Rouge, China promised to stop assisting the Communist Party of Thailand, which had been fighting an insurgency against the government in Bangkok since the mid 1960s.

Within days, Chinese weapons began flowing to the Khmer Rouge and before long the group's old guerrilla bases were operational once more. By 1980, the Khmer Rouge fielded an army of about 35,000 troops, had about 100,000 people under its control and was back on the offensive. On the diplomatic front, it still retained its seat at the United Nations General Assembly as the legitimate government of Cambodia, while the Vietnamese-installed government of the People's Republic of Kampuchea (PRK) was an outlawed regime to most of the international community. Slapped with international sanctions, the PRK was cut off from most of the world, while the Khmer Rouge found newfound friends with non-communist Southeast Asia and the West.

In 1982, the Khmer Rouge entered a coalition government with two non-communist Cambodian resistance groups and formed a broad alliance against the Vietnamese. This group, called the Coalition Government of Democratic Kampuchea (CGDK), held Cambodia's seat at the UN until 1991 and received an estimated US$1.3 billion dollars in aid throughout the 1980s from China, the United States, Thailand, Malaysia and Singapore. The Khmer Rouge was the largest military benefactor of the group and therefore received the bulk of this aid. Most of the aid came from China (about $1 billion) while funds from the US, Thailand, Malaysia and Singapore were directed at the two non-communist factions of the group. Pol Pot, Ieng Sary and all the Khmer Rouge's high officials retained top leadership positions within the CGDK and no non-communists were given responsible roles in the group. In addition to the massive amount of foreign aid it received, the Khmer Rouge faction of the group controlled much of the cross border trade between Cambodia and Thailand. Hence, it was through Cold War politics and capitalist enterprising that the most radical communist group in history was brought back from the dead.

In its rebirth, however, the Khmer Rouge tried to distance itself from the ideology that it took to such an extreme when it was in power. In 1981, the movement officially renounced communism and dissolved its Communist Party of Kampuchea (CPK), making the CPK the first and only communist party in history to dissolve itself. The goal of communism was abandoned and instead efforts were focused on the task of winning back the country from the Vietnamese. Social restrictions imposed during the Khmer Rouge's reign were relaxed, if not altogether lifted. Communal living and collective eating, a fundamental aspect of Democratic Kampuchea, ended as did the ban on personal possessions and private enterprise. People with skills such as being able to speak a foreign language were no longer executed, but put to use. People were given second chances instead of fatal blows to the head. But old habits die hard, even for mass murderers. The malignant organs of the Khmer Rouge were never removed and would continually re-emerge in one pestilent form or another until the very end.

Pol Pot remained the supreme leader of the movement with his murderous clique from Democratic Kampuchea retaining top leadership positions; tyranny still prevailed. In the Khmer Rouge guerrilla camps inside Cambodia and along the Thai border, strict rules were imposed which sacrificed the individual for the collective; totalitarianism prevailed and indoctrination continued through study sessions, isolation, restriction on movement, and fear. Although more moderate, the Khmer Rouge was still a dangerous group whose radicalism had not been completely eradicated, it was only lying dormant.

This radicalism resurfaced in full force in the 1990s following the Vietnamese withdrawal from Cambodia in 1989. The withdrawal was followed two years later with a UN-brokered Peace Agreement and, shortly later, the largest UN peacekeeping operation in history. In full breach of the Agreement, the Khmer Rouge refused to disarm, and refused to be monitored by the UN. Instead it militarily expanded its territory during the so-called 'peace process'. It also boycotted the UN-sponsored elections in 1993 and threw the country back into civil war. But with the Cold War over and the rank and file of the movement tired of a lifetime of fighting, the Khmer Rouge found itself both internationally isolated and becoming increasingly unpopular at home. As defections increased and peasant resentment grew, it fell back on the radicalism and brutality of its past.

By 1994, a deliberate policy of terror was launched once more. For years the Khmer Rouge had kidnapped and killed both civil and military authorities in the areas it had infiltrated, but now it began to target the general civilian population for attack. Its tactics included the systematic destruction of enemy-controlled villages and rice fields, the abduction of villagers for ransom or forced labor, looting, rape, murder, the massacre of Vietnamese, and the kidnap and killing of foreigners. In addition, the Khmer Rouge began to harden its economic and social policies in areas under its control; among these policies was the banning and confiscation of privately owned means of transport, an order reminiscent of its days in power. In some areas, communal eating was re-imposed and private trade was banned.

The movement's socialist roots were being replanted, but few outside the hard-line leadership wanted to re-sow the seeds of the past. The movement was therefore beginning to fragment and defections became prevalent.

The biggest split came in August 1996. Ieng Sary, the foreign minister of Democratic Kampuchea, led a breakaway faction of about 4,000 soldiers from the group's northwestern strongholds of Pailin and Phnom Malai near the Thai border. Not only did this defection reduce the Khmer Rouge's troop strength by nearly half, but it brought with it the economic heartland of the movement. The regions he took were rich in timber and gems and provided the group with several million dollars a month in revenue; their loss was an economic deathblow to the Khmer Rouge. The toughening of policies by the hardliners in Anlong Veng, such as the attempt to re-impose the collectivization of property and the banning of private transport—from ox carts to cars—was a major factor behind the defections. The split was the biggest set back for the Khmer Rouge since 1979 and crippled the movement to the point of no recovery. The end was near.

The following June, still furious at the loss of Pailin and Phnom Malai, Pol Pot summoned one of his division commanders and told him to 'take care' of the man he believed to be responsible for the loss of those bases. The man was Son Sen, Pol Pot's former defense minister and friend of 40 years. Within hours, Son Sen was dead. In an act of typical Khmer Rouge brutality, Son Sen's wife and 13 other family members and aids were also murdered. It was one atrocity too many. Within days, Ta Mok seized control from Pol Pot and sent the 71-year-old despot fleeing for his life. He was captured a few days later and sentenced to life in prison by a bizarre people's tribunal. He died peacefully in his sleep ten months later, on 15 April 1998, on top of the Dangrek Escarpment, where Mok's forces were pinned down.

The day after I acquired the photograph of Pol Pot in late April 1998, RCAF soldiers showed me around much of Anlong Veng and brought me to the deserted homes of Khmer Rouge leaders Ta Mok and Khieu Samphan. A group of Khmer Rouge defectors were on the way down the mountain to surrender to the government that day, so RCAF soldiers eased up on their artillery assaults, which gave them time to give me a personal tour of the town.

In many ways the town was like a museum—except that its artifacts were up for grabs. Photographs of Khmer Rouge leaders, notebooks, documents, and schoolbooks were just some of the interesting historical items left behind during the exodus from Anlong Veng. There were also the buildings, such as the town's school, meeting hall, the hospital, and homes of the leaders, all providing a rare and fascinating insight into life under the Khmer Rouge. While a lot of the town had already been looted by soldiers, many items and materials remained in place. In the town's school, for example, the blackboards weren't even erased.

'Bad-smelling meat or any enemies within our lines must be absolutely destroyed,' was written on one of them. 'Struggle hard against internal and external national enemies' and 'learn how to conduct hit and run warfare' were classroom messages for how to be a good leader.

One of the first places I was shown that day was the deserted house of Ta Mok. His compound overlooked the town's picturesque lake, which Mok himself had helped to develop by building dikes around it to maintain a steadier water level all year round. Known as 'Mok's Water', it looked more like a marsh than a lake, with verdant islands dotting the water and dead trees rising from below. A sign near the water warned people not to fish with explosives, for such people are 'youn' (the derogatory term for Vietnamese) who, according to Mok, 'must have their throats cut'. This directive was issued the previous December, according to Khmer Rouge documents later discovered on top of the escarpment. Another directive issued at the same time concerned people who started forest fires: they were to be burned alive.

Mok's teak house, with two floors and a bunker-type basement, was by far the nicest and biggest in the town. It was decorated with Angkorian carvings and large mural paintings of nature scenes and Cambodian temples. What struck me the most, however, was a large mural map of Cambodia that depicted southern Vietnam as Cambodian territory that was stolen by the Vietnamese. Even as the Khmer Rouge was reduced to controlling one last sliver of territory in Cambodia, it was still obsessed with regaining territory that the Vietnamese had taken centuries before—the same obsession that ultimately led to the defeat of the regime by the Vietnamese in 1979.

There were two other houses in the compound, apparently used as guest residences for Mok's visitors, plus an outhouse and a small shelter, perhaps used for storage. At the front of the compound was an old rundown truck, probably damaged in the fighting that month, which seemed to symbolize the state of Mok's forces about 15 kilometers away on top of the Dangrek Escarpment.

A short walk away from Mok's compound were the much smaller and simpler homes of other Khmer Rouge leaders, including the former head of state, Khieu Samphan. Like many of the movement's leadership, including Ieng Sary, Son Sen and Pol Pot, Samphan was educated in France in the 1950s, which was essentially where the roots of the Khmer Rouge began. It was in France where these men and a handful of other Khmer students formed the radical political beliefs, bonds, alliances and friendships that would later wreak havoc upon their homeland. It was also in France that these men developed intellectually, earning diplomas and degrees, thus making them some of the most educated leaders in the history of Asian communism. It doesn't take an intellectual to see the disturbing irony: that the leaders of one of history's most radical and brutal revolutions were highly educated men.

None was more educated than Khieu Samphan. He studied in France and received a doctorate degree from the University of Paris. Samphan was considered the Khmer Rouge's leading intellectual. His 1959 PhD thesis, entitled 'Cambodia's Economy and Industrial Development', argued that Cambodia had to become self-sufficient and end its economic dependency on the developed world—a notion that became the economic cornerstone of the failed Khmer Rouge revolution.

After the collapse of the regime, Samphan became the foreign voice of the movement and Pol Pot appointed him its nominal leader in 1985, although the despot still called the shots. In the CGDK, the tripartite coalition government in exile formed in 1982, Samphan was the vice minister responsible for foreign affairs—the only position that mattered for a government in exile. He later represented the Khmer Rouge in the peace negotiations that led to the signing of the Paris Peace Agreement in October 1991. When he came to Phnom Penh the following month to inaugurate the Khmer Rouge's mission in the capital as part of the accords (under the Peace Agreement, a temporary government was established comprising representatives of the incumbent government led by Hun Sen and delegates from the factions that had been opposing it), Samphan was mobbed and beaten by members of Hun Sen's security forces. Needless to say, his time in Phnom Penh was short.

Samphan was loyal to Pol Pot until the very end, even taking his side when he had Son Sen and his wife killed in June 1997. But with the despot's demise that month, Samphan had no other choice but to side with Mok, leaving his mountain home on the escarpment near the home of Pol Pot for a bamboo hut in Anlong Veng near to that of Mok.

Rummaging through his home in Anlong Veng gave me a lesson in more than just war looting. Scattered throughout his one-room home were piles of papers and academic books in no less than five different languages, including English, French, German, Vietnamese and Russian. The scene struck me. Here was the home of one of the top leaders of one of the most radical and brutal revolutionary movements the world has ever known—and it was the home of a highly educated man. It was the home of a man who could have chosen any path in life, and he chose the path of a peasant revolutionary. Living out his later years in jungle hideouts and huts, Samphan was clearly a man who dedicated his life to a revolution in which he believed. The Khmer Rouge can be accused of many horrific things, but one thing they cannot be accused of is lack of commitment. One can fault their revolution and deplore their ways, but it is difficult to doubt their dedication to their cause.

I acquired two more historic photographs that day: one of Khieu Samphan dining with Norodom Sihanouk (who was reinstated as king in 1993) and Sihanouk's wife, Monineath (a picture most likely taken in Thailand in the 1980s); the other was of Pol Pot, Ieng Sary and Son Sen, which was most likely taken in China in the early 1980s. However, the most precious artifact I took away that day was not a picture or any other tangible object, but the historic words of an RCAF commander that have been permanently stored in the archives of my mind. Earlier in the day, I accompanied a tank unit for another artillery assault into the Dangrek Mountains where Mok's forces were pinned down—and where Samphan was also believed to be. But after setting up position, the assault was called off because a group of Khmer Rouge guerrillas had surrendered to the government. While this wasn't a defection that would signal the end of the conflict, it was one more blow to a movement that couldn't afford to take any more hits. It was clear that the Khmer Rouge was a diminished force incapable of mounting a comeback. For one RCAF commander, however, Cambodia's civil war had finally come to an end. 'I

am so happy,' he told me, with a smile th̶
fierceness from his battle-hardened face.
finally come to my country.'

As the fighting subsided, I left Anlong Veng
next day to get to Bangkok as quickly as possible
try and sell my pictures. I hitched a lift on the same
Russian truck which had brought me, as it was heading
on another supply run. It was an uneventful journey.
We came back to the refugee camp at O'Bai Tap, then
on to Siem Reap where I enjoyed my first good meal
in days, before I hired a moto-taxi to take me to the
Thai border. Arriving just after the border had closed
for the day, I spent the night on the Cambodian side
in the dusty town of Poipet, where I collected my
thoughts over two bottles of ice-cold beer. I can't recall
what those thoughts were, but I can still feel that
glowing high of alcohol and happiness from making
it to Anlong Veng, seeing a part of history unfold, and
returning to the luxury of life outside of a war zone.

The next day in Bangkok I sold the three pictures of
Pol Pot and Khieu Samphan to the Associated Press
for $75 each. The excitement of my first journalism
sale soon wore off after I received a phone call at the
reception of my guest house from Rob Mountfort, the
photo editor of the *Far Eastern Economic Review*. 'Hey,
great job of getting that picture of Pol Pot,' he told me.
'But you screwed up. You could have gotten $10,000
for it.' I was left to dwell on my disappointment in the
decadent surroundings of Bangkok.

I returned to Anlong Veng just over a month later, in early June 1998, with another Canadian freelance journalist who was living in Cambodia, George McLeod. Young, gung-ho, and eager for adventure, George and I quickly became good friends and opted to travel to Anlong Veng on a more independent and reliable mode of transport than moto-taxis and military vehicles, namely, motorbikes.

With little thought and even less planning, we rented two Honda off-road bikes at a shop in Phnom Penh, leaving our passports as collateral and telling the owner we were just going to take the bikes on a leisurely ride to the beach. The plan was simple: ride to Siem Reap the first day (about 300 kilometers northwest of the capital), spend the night at a cheap guest house, then retrace the route I took in April, first to the refugee camp at O' Bai Tap, then into the jungle trails that lead to Anlong Veng. Our goal for the trip was equally simple, 'get shit'; and by 'shit' we meant Khmer Rouge paraphernalia, such as photographs (I was still fuming over the missed $10,000 on the Pol Pot photo and was hoping to find more), as well as information.

It was a grueling two-day ride—much more grueling than we anticipated—especially the last leg of the journey from O'Bai Tap to government-controlled Anlong Veng. With the annual monsoon rains beginning to fall, the jungle passage was quickly turning into a river of mud. It was an arduous challenge that fully tested out motorbike skills (which we had little) and our fear (which we had plenty). Desperately trying to maneuver through the punishing terrain, and unsure at times if we were on the right path or riding straight into rebel territory, the 60 kilometer ride from O'bai Tap to Anlong Veng took us about six hours, leaving us in a state of physical and mental exhaustion by the time we reached government positions in the town late in the afternoon. As difficult as it was, this was nothing compared to our journey back a few days later.

When we arrived into Anlong Veng and after we arranged a place to sleep at the same quarters in which I stayed in April, we headed down to the town's lake. Its murky, swampy water did little to deter us from jumping in and washing our filth-coated bodies from the day's journey.

'Do you think there are any dead bodies in here?' George asked me.

'Yes, probably,' I replied.

Needless to say, it was a quick bath.

The next day, George and I set out on our bikes to reach the frontlines. The RCAF had made significant advances since I was last there, with the government now controlling the entire road to the Thai border. In early May, just days after I had left, RCAF soldiers dislodged the guerrillas from their main base on the escarpment, Mountain 200, forcing Mok's dwindling forces to flee westwards. Just before the fall of the mountain, at least 15,000 civilians and unarmed soldiers fled into Thailand, indicating that the number of rebels was much higher than the estimated 200 to 500 previously reckoned by the government. But it didn't matter. The rebels were getting overrun, and furthermore, running out of territory into which to run.

The next day, George and I made our way north to Mountain 200 of the Dangrek Escarpment, and the Sa-ngam border pass 15 kilometers north of the town. The smooth dirt road to the border was a rare Khmer Rouge success story, being one of the best roads in the entire country. Anlong Veng also boasted one of the best hospitals outside of Phnom Penh, a striking fact that I immediately noticed when I first arrived in the town in April. Although riddled with bullet holes from the recent fighting, the building stood out as the biggest and nicest in Anlong Veng—much nicer than any other hospital I had seen in rural Cambodia. In terms of infrastructure and healthcare, Anlong Veng was actually a well-off Cambodian town. But in terms of personal freedom and quality of life, it was merely another Cambodian killing field.

The area was still deserted except for government soldiers, a trickle of civilians who had begun returning to the town and the district, and a few hardcore migrants from nearby areas who came to take advantage of Cambodia's newest marketplace. One such migrant was a man from Siem Reap who opened a tiny stall outside of the main RCAF compound in the town, selling canned food, instant noodles, drinks, and a handful of basic supplies for the soldiers. While I'm sure he only made a few dollars a day, I admired his entrepreneurial spirit in opening Anlong Veng's first convenience store.

Lush green crop fields flanked the road all the way to the escarpment, which was indicative of the area's rich, fertile soil, while nearby forests and piles of felled trees highlighted the lucrative timber trade that for years had been the economic lifeline of the Khmer Rouge at Anlong Veng. However, the industry had taken a hit over the past two years when Thailand began stemming the trade under considerable international pressure. By the spring of 1998, there were millions of dollars of stockpiled logs simply rotting away in Anlong Veng.

George and I cruised through the area, passing deserted hamlets and encountering the odd soldier or civilian, before beginning the steep ascent up the mountain road to the top of the escarpment. About half way up the mountain there was a strange boulder in the middle of the road; under its overhang were four stone carvings of soldiers and workers, giving the impression that they were carrying the weight of the boulder on their shoulders. It was built in the early 1990s but received an alteration in May 1998 by RCAF soldiers who were advancing through the area: three of the stone carvings had their heads chopped off and one was missing a leg. It was actually quite funny.

Once atop the mountain, George and I were welcomed by RCAF soldiers who then filled us in on the current situation. Fighting had subsided and the government was firmly in control of the area, while Khmer Rouge forces were about 20 kilometers to the west. We were at a place called Sa-ngam Pass; a lone T-54 tank was parked nearby. A few meters away was the border checkpoint that marked the boundary between Cambodia and Thailand. While the border was closed to foreigners, Thai soldiers walked freely across and mingled with their Cambodian counterparts, who had taken control of the pass just a few weeks before.

Sa-ngam Pass is the final resting place of Pol Pot, although if past deeds dictate after death demeanour, he's certainly not resting. While the cause of death remains uncertain, the official account is that he died of heart failure at 11:15pm on 15 April 1998. He was cremated on a pile of rubbish and tires a few days later, exiting the world fittingly.

An autopsy was never performed and there were many peculiar circumstances surrounding his death. These included the timing—he died perhaps days or even hours ahead of being possibly seized by US officials in order to be prosecuted for war crimes, certainly something the remaining Khmer Rouge leaders would not have wanted; the fact that he was fully dressed when his body was shown to journalists the next day, despite the Khmer Rouge claiming he had died in his sleep; the slight revisions of the details of his death by his jailor; and the fact that he was immediately embalmed with about three gallons of formalin—an unusual chemical to have in such quantity at a remote guerrilla camp. Peculiarities aside, we mustn't forget he was also a weak old man suffering from a variety of ailments. Perhaps it was simply the case that his time had come.

Anxious to see his cremation site, George and I asked certain RCAF soldiers for directions. As one of the soldiers had a primitive metal detector which was used for detecting landmines, George was quick to ask him if he would like to accompany us. He willingly agreed and hopped on the back of George's bike. As we set out along a narrow trail into the mine-infested area, George turned to him and said, 'Feel free to stop me at any time if you want to get off the bike and use your metal detector. I don't mind.' At the time it wasn't funny, but to this day we can't recall the story without bursting into laughter.

The cremation site was just a few hundred meters away from the border check point. It was literally just a pile of trash, bits of tire here, a rag there; a motley jumble of refuse in a small clearing which marked the grave of Cambodia's deliverer of death.

Before his arrest the previous June, Pol Pot lived about nine kilometers east of the pass, at a jungle hideout atop the escarpment at a place called Kbal Ansoang. He moved there in 1994 and lived within walking distance of his most trusted followers, including Khieu Samphan. His modest brick house, surrounded and hidden by thick jungle and bamboo, stood at the edge of the escarpment and overlooked the plains around Anlong Veng which stretched southwards to Angkor. It was a beautiful view from a tranquil jungle setting adorned with ponds, streams and waterfalls. It was a place more fitting for a philosopher than a mass killer, except for the nearby minefields perhaps.

About seven kilometers to the west of Pol Pot's jungle refuge were the houses of other top ranking Khmer Rouge leaders. Known as the 'Middle Houses', for their position between Kbal Ansoang and the Sangam Pass, the cluster of dwellings included those of Noun Chea, Son Sen and Ta Mok.

During the Khmer Rouge regime, Noun Chea was Pol Pot's right hand man, 'Brother Number Two', while Son Sen was considered number four in the hierarchy. He was minister of defense and was responsible for the country's internal security. The two were also members of Pol Pot's three-member ultra secret Security Committee responsible for the suppression of internal dissent, and thus played a key role in directing the horrors of S-21, the regime's infamous interrogation center. It was here at the 'Middle Houses' where Son Sen, his wife, and 13 of his family members and aids were killed in June 1997, which ultimately signaled Pol Pot's fall from grace. He never displayed remorse nor expressed regret for the death and destruction he visited upon Cambodia, and he took his denial of wrongdoing to the grave.

After exploring the area around Pol Pot's cremation site, George and I decided to risk venturing farther west towards Khmer Rouge lines. We asked the soldier with the landmine detector if he would join us and he happily agreed. We got back on our bikes and rode into the jungle on a narrow mountain trail. George and I would take turns riding in the front to take equal share of the risk of hitting a landmine. Pushing our fear to the limit, we rode slowly; the person in the front taking most of the risk while the person at the back stayed far enough behind to hopefully avoid being hit should the front man detonate a mine. The going was slow, and at several times our RCAF landmine detector would tell us to stop so he could check for mines.

'Take your time,' we would tell him, encouraging him to do his job properly, for our lives and limbs depended on the quality of his work. Luckily for us, he was pretty good at his trade.

I'll never forget the eeriness of the jungle as we rode through it, its dreadful serenity, or the strange orchestra produced from a combination of the sound of the forest and the engines of our motorbikes. We passed deserted Khmer Rouge campsites, an improvised mine rigged to a tree, and small bands of RCAF soldiers securing their newly captured territory. I didn't know what George was thinking, but I certainly didn't want to be the one to say we should stop and go back. Instead, we kept going, slowly winding our way through the mine-infested forest, resisting the common sense instinct which told us to stop. I can still picture George riding on the back edge of his bike, his arms stretched out to hold the handlebars, as if that extra distance would save him from the blast of a landmine. And I remember copying him, thinking what a great idea it was, impervious to common sense and basic physics.

We eventually reached a small clearing in the jungle where a unit of RCAF soldiers was stationed. It was the vanguard of the RCAF in the area, the last base that separated government positions from the Khmer Rouge, perhaps ten kilometers away. It wasn't much of a camp, just a small base with a few temporary huts and shelters. With much of the heavy fighting finished, the soldiers were resting and relaxing, some asleep in hammocks swung across trees. We inquired about the trail to the west and whether it was possible to continue on towards Khmer Rouge positions. With the rebel group on the verge of collapse, George and I desperately wanted to meet with its soldiers and leaders face to face to finally see for ourselves this secretive group that we had heard about and read about, but had never met. Were they really sadistic monsters who would execute us just for being foreigners? I wasn't convinced, and neither was George. After rummaging through Khieu Samphan's house just over a month before, and seeing the books he read, realizing he was a highly educated man, I didn't believe he would just shoot us if we rode up to their jungle hideout. In fact, I wanted to talk to him, to ask him questions, to hear his side of the story. I also believed (and still do) in the goodness of people, and that if we rode up to some young Khmer Rouge soldiers, they would be just as friendly as their RCAF enemies. The day I searched through Samphan's house in April, I also met one of the Khmer Rouge defectors who came down the mountain that day. We shook hands and smiled at each other. As far as I could tell, he was a nice guy. Perhaps all of this was foolish and naïve thinking, and that the group responsible for sending 1.7 million people to their graves would not think twice about sending two more.

In the end though, it was the landmines that halted our progress. We repeatedly consulted the RCAF soldiers at that forward base about continuing on, and they repeatedly responded with one word, 'mines'. Even our landmine detector friend refused to go any farther. We were at the end of the line.

Disappointed, but satisfied at our effort, we rode back to the border post at the Sa-ngam Pass where we were delayed by some Thai and RCAF soldiers and a bottle of rice wine. We shared a few shots with the soldiers, calming our nerves after the jungle ride, until the afternoon sun dimmed into dusk, giving us our cue to get on our bikes and ride back to our sleeping quarters at the RCAF command post in Anlong Veng. It was an exhilarating day, and sleep was the perfect antidote to our fear-induced high.

We spent the next morning in and around the town before we set off into the jungle back to O'Bai Tap and Siem Reap. While I didn't do too well on the paraphernalia aspect of our 'get shit' goal of the trip (as I didn't find any more rare photographs of Pol Pot and/or other Khmer Rouge leaders), George came away with a Khmer Rouge school textbook and one of Pol Pot's t-shirts. As for information, what we got was quite clear: the government was firmly in control of Anlong Veng and its surrounding area, Khmer Rouge forces were in disarray and all but spent as a fighting force, and Cambodia's decades-old civil war was virtually over. Like the dirt that churned beneath our wheels as we left Anlong Veng, it was little more than dust in the wind.

It was late morning and a light drizzle was beginning to fall as we rode into the jungle; the monsoon rains were threatening to unleash their fury upon us. It was clear from the beginning that the rains had taken their toll on the trail since we rode up from O'Bai Tap. Parts of it were now almost impossible to get through, composed of drowning mud that almost devoured our bikes. Slick rocks, ice-like dirt, heavy sand, waist-deep mud, and fallen trees lined the trail like a series of booby-traps. At times we had to struggle for every meter, forcing, muscling, and willing our way through the relentless terrain of the rain-soaked jungle, bruising bike and body alike, beating one section only to get slammed by the next. We would spin out, tail out, flip out, wipe out, get up, fall down, shout, scream, laugh, curse, rest, ride, rant; it was road rage at its worst, except without the road.

Daylight was beginning to dim. We were out of water, exhausted, and the refugee camp at O'Bai Tap was still nowhere in sight. Suddenly, the one thing that we didn't want happening happened: George's bike broke down. There was no warning, no crash, no rattle, no pop; it just gave out. There was still plenty of petrol and everything seemed in working order. The bike simply refused to start. With darkness rapidly descending upon the jungle canopy, we decided it was best to abandon it. We pushed it off the trail and attempted to hide it behind some bushes, hoping it would be safe for the night until we came back for it the next day. With George on the back of my bike, we continued on, desperately trying to get out of the jungle before dark. Unbelievably, we only progressed a few hundred meters before mine did the exact same thing. A bad day just got worse.

Being out of options and unprepared to spend the night in the jungle, we abandoned my bike as well and continued on foot. By now it was pouring rain, but the fury of the monsoon was nothing compared to the fury that raged inside of us. And just as it seemed things could not possibly get any worse, I slipped off a makeshift bridge and fell into a swamp. I screamed out of anger and cursed like a crazed man.

'There's no point in getting angry and calling the swamp names,' George told me, trying to calm me down. 'You're cleaner now than you were before.'

To illustrate his point, George jumped in the swamp with me.

All of the day's misfortune was soon reversed when we walked around a bend in the trail, no more than a kilometer from our deserted bikes, and saw the beautiful image of blue plastic tarps in the distance. O'Bai Tap, home to some 4,000 refugees, received two more arrivals that evening.

'Water, water, we need water,' we begged the refugees, using our limited knowledge of Khmer combined with hand motions of frantically pouring an imaginary drink into our mouths. We went up to the shelter of an elderly woman, who immediately burst into laughter. She couldn't stop laughing as she gave us a pot of water, which we poured down our grit-coated faces and into our parching mouths. Suddenly, it seemed as if the entire population of the camp descended upon us. Everyone was laughing—a rare occurrence among the typically demure and submissive Cambodians accustomed to living under Khmer Rouge control. We were the laughing stock of the camp; our bodies were coated with mud and filth unlike any refugee they'd ever seen, we came stumbling into their place of sanctuary, begging them for water and help, which made them roar with laughter, as if they were thinking, 'so you guys thought you were tough—we've been doing this for the past 30 years and we don't even have motorbikes.' It wasn't until later that we realized the irony of two foreigners begging for help at a refugee camp.

After making our way through the camp, we managed to find a pickup truck with a driver who was willing to take us to Siem Reap. He demanded $50, a ridiculously high price for the 60 kilometer or so ride, but he knew we were in no position to decline.

'$30,' we bargained with him.

'No, $50,' he replied.

'$40,' we snapped back.

'$50,' he responded.

When it was clear that he wasn't going to take us for much less, we offered him $49. He still didn't budge. We settled at $50—what the average Cambodian made in about two months of work.

We got in the truck and enjoyed a nice, smooth ride through the darkness of ancient Angkor before arriving in Siem Reap. Soon we were at a nice, comfortable guesthouse enjoying a hot meal and some cold beer along with some other young foreigners who had come to town to explore the nearby temples.

'Where have you guys been?' one of them asked us.

'Anlong Veng,' we replied.

'Anlong Veng, I've never heard of it. What's there?' he asked.

Not wanting to engage in a long conversation with an ignorant backpacker, George just smiled at him and replied, 'There's a really nice waterfall.'

Khmer Rouge forces held out along the rugged terrain between the Cambodian and Thai border for several more months, but surviving as nothing more than a shadow of its blood-soaked past. Finally, on 4 December 1998, the last core group of several hundred rebels agreed to surrender to the government, effectively ending Cambodia's 30-year war and burying the casket of the Khmer Rouge. On Christmas Day, 20 years to the day since Vietnam invaded and ended their reign of terror, Khieu Samphan and Noun Chea emerged from the jungle to surrender, giving up a lifetime of revolution making. The only one left was Ta Mok, who remained at large until he was captured by government forces in March 1999.

In a bizarre welcome-back gesture to the society they once tried to destroy, Khieu Samphan and Noun Chea were treated by the government to a beach holiday and a trip to the temples of Angkor. At a press conference in Phnom Penh on 29 December 1998, Khieu Samphan urged his compatriots to 'let bygones be bygones', while Noun Chea made this peculiar, if not cynical, apology, 'Actually, we are very sorry not only for the lives of the people of Cambodia, but even for the lives of all animals that suffered because of the war.'

With the death of the Khmer Rouge, even the lives of Cambodia's animals improved.

CHAPTER 2

BURMA:

THE KAREN'S ENDLESS STRUGGLE

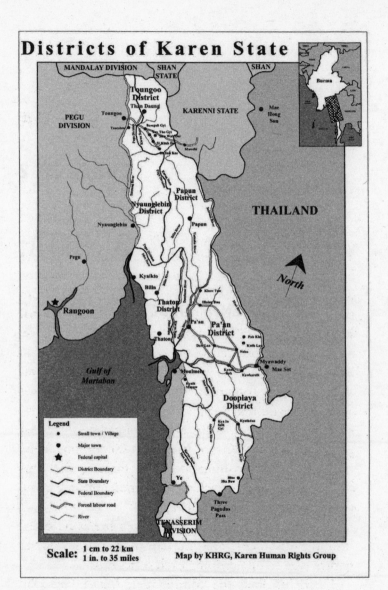

Districts of Karen State

MANDALAY DIVISION

SHAN STATE

SHAN

Burma

Toungoo District

Than Daung

PEGU DIVISION

Toungoo

Tantabin

Bawgali Gyi

Tha Gyi

Sho Wah Der

Si Kheh Der

Bu Sah Kee

KARENNI STATE

Maw chi

Mae Hong Son

THAILAND

Papun District

Nyaunglebin District

Nyaunglebin

Papun

Pegu

Kyaikto

Bilin

Khew Tue

Hsiny Wee

North

Thaton District

Rangoon

Pa'an

 Pa'an District

Pah Klu

Kwih Lu

Thaton

Daw Lan

Nabu

Moulmein

Kaser-doh

Kawkareik

Myawaddy

Mae Sot

Gulf of Martaban

Kyah Inn

Seik

Dooplaya District

Kya In Seik Gyi

Kyaikdon

Legend

• Small town / Village

● Major town

★ Federal capital

〰 District Boundary

〰 State Boundary

〰 Federal Boundary

〰 Forced labour road

〰 River

Ye

Hwe Hta Baw

Three Pagodas Pass

TENASSERIM DIVISION

Scale: 1 cm to 22 km
1 in. to 35 miles

Map by KHRG, Karen Human Rights Group

BURMA

The view from the mountaintop in the jungle was beautiful. The verdant hills that spread out across the horizon painted a picture that seemed out of place from the vantage point of a guerrilla camp. The occasional sound of engines could be heard in the distance, reminding me how close we were to Thailand, as in this part of Burma there were only jungle trails. It was an ideal setting for a mountain resort, but no one was going to make that happen any time soon. For now, the only settlement in the area belonged to the 201st battalion of the Karen National Liberation Army (KNLA), whose commander was making the final preparations for an attack on a Burmese military camp that was a few kilometers away.

'Nature is so beautiful,' he said to me as he gazed into the distance from his hammock. 'But human nature isn't. We are wiping each other out.'

I had first met the commander, Major Ner Dah Mya, in August 2000 when I came to the Thai-Burmese border area to report on the Karen's armed struggle against the Burmese army, which was in its 52nd year. Despite being ill-equipped and outnumbered, and having unbearable hardships inflicted upon their people at the hands of one of the world's most repressive military regimes, the KNLA refused to surrender and bow down to oppression. This was an army I had to see.

My goal was to document the Karen's struggle and, more specifically, to photograph the KNLA in combat. To do this I moved to the town of Mae Sot on the Thai-Burmese border, bought an off-road motorbike and drove several times a week to Ner Dah's base camp, which was located about 50 kilometers away. I would park my bike in the nearby Thai village of Padi before walking a kilometer to the rebel's camp at Walaykey on the Burmese side of the frontier.

After three months of cultivating ties with Ner Nah and his soldiers, earning their friendship and respect by visiting them on an almost daily basis and bringing them much-needed supplies, I received word from a Karen friend of mine named Tennyson that a guerrilla attack was imminent.

I awoke early the next morning, arriving at Walaykey just in time to accompany the departing soldiers on what turned out to be a five-day operation. Their mission was to attack a Burmese position called Tojo, which was manned by about 30 government soldiers. They aimed to capture the position, loot it for arms and ammunition, burn it down, and then retreat—a typical hit-and-run guerrilla operation.

From his mountaintop hideout, Ner Dah's battalion readied itself for attack. Food rations were distributed and ammunition was divided up and given out sparingly. Weapons were cleaned, checked and loaded. Reconnaissance of the nearby area revealed that the Burmese were contained in their position at Tojo and were not patrolling the surrounding jungle—in other words, they were easy targets for the KNLA. After several days camped on the mountain, orders were given to move out and push forward towards Tojo.

It was the early morning and I had just spent my third night on the mountain with the guerrillas. My eyes had become infected from my constant use of contact lenses without cleaning them properly but my eyes were the least of my concerns. Readied for battle, I took pictures of the soldiers as they lined up, prayed and received words of encouragement from their leader before proceeding into the jungle towards the enemy camp. They were armed with automatic weapons, mortars, heavy machine guns, and rocket-propelled grenades. I followed them armed with two Nikon cameras and an inordinate supply of adrenaline.

I was completely focused as we moved cautiously through the jungle, fully aware that the enemy could be waiting to ambush us at any bend along the trail. However, it was impossible for me not to be distracted by the amazing show of determination from the group: there were porters wearing flip-flops carrying mortar shells in bamboo baskets strapped to their backs; a 13-year-old boy whose M-16 was almost as big as he was; and a trail full of hardcore soldiers willing to fight and die for their people. 'Revolution', said Tennyson, 'is the life of the Karen people.'

Tennyson was not an average Karen guerrilla. He had shoulder-length hair, a house in Mae Sot, and drove a Harley-like chopper. He would commute to the war on a part-time basis, volunteering his fighting skills when they were needed, such as during the attack on Tojo, then return to Thailand where he dabbled in a variety of business ventures. I hung out with him quite a bit in Mae Sot and he would tell me fascinating stories, like how he used to roam the waters off the coast of Burma in the 'KNLA's Navy', collecting taxes and avoiding Burmese gun ships. More inspirational than this was the time he came face to face with a Burmese soldier during a fierce jungle battle in 1985. The soldier pulled his trigger before Tennyson could pull his, but the soldier's weapon jammed. With Tennyson ready to fire, the soldier surrendered and begged for his life even though he had just killed two of Tennyson's friends. Tennyson was carefully contemplating pulling the trigger. He was consumed by rage and thought about all the friends and family that had been killed by Burmese soldiers, men just like him, but he also thought about the Bible and particularly of the verse, 'love your enemies'.

'I was shaking,' Tennyson recounted to me, 'I was thinking that "love your enemies" is bullshit. I wanted to cancel that verse from the Bible. But in the end, I surrendered to God.' Tennyson, with tears rolling down his face, told the soldier not to be afraid, that he would not kill him. He also told his friends not to harm him and, after assuring him he would be safe, escorted him out of rebel territory into Thailand and to an office of the United Nations High Commission for Refugees. Today, according to Tennyson, the soldier lives in the West. Since then, Tennyson says he has helped at least 70 other Burmese prisoners make it to Thailand alive. 'It's not that we want to kill,' he told me about his people's struggle, 'we just want freedom.'

We approached the enemy camp at Tojo in the midafternoon after a slow and arduous ascent up the mountain. Ner Dah assembled a scout team of six or so soldiers which was to penetrate the front entrance of the camp. The team was led by him and included Tennyson; they also signalled for me to accompany them. Although I didn't know what to expect, I was eager not to miss out on any action, so I gladly complied. I stayed in the middle of the column and was careful to plant my feet in the exact footprints of the person in front of me in order to reduce my chances of stepping on an enemy landmine.

Without being spotted by Burmese sentries, we entered the front of the camp and took cover in a trench which the Burmese had built for defending it. Ironically, their own defense system was now being used against them. With the Burmese soldiers about 300 meters into their main compound and the front entrance of the camp successfully secured by Ner Dah's men, orders were given for the rest of the battalion to move in and take up positions. Just as I was beginning to relax in the safety of the trench, Ner Dah handed me a sniper rifle and told me he'd be back later. Without much thought I took it, but as he disappeared beyond the trench-line I suddenly realized I was all alone with 30 enemy soldiers nearby. In the fear and confusion I remember thinking to myself, 'If Burmese soldiers come, do I shoot them with my camera or the rifle?' Luckily, I didn't have to make that choice. KNLA soldiers soon appeared and Ner Dah returned shortly afterwards to take back his rifle.

It was nearing dusk and Ner Dah's battalion of some 200 guerrillas were all within firing distance of the main compound where approximately 30 Burmese soldiers were going about their daily routine. They were completely unaware of their camp's fatal breach of security. Later in the night, as the Karen guerrillas used the cover of darkness to set up their 81mm mortars and heavy machine guns for a dawn attack, we could hear the Burmese soldiers laughing and singing. For the first time in three months with the Karen I finally saw the human side of their hated enemy. It was surreal. In fact, the entire night was surreal as we camped down in a Burmese bunker waiting for the dawn, listening to the sounds and voices of the Burmese soldiers, watching the full moon that lit up the sky: such a beautiful night of sights and sounds that suffocated the senses. One Karen soldier, a friend of mine named Ge Ge, looked towards the Burmese compound and said in an almost apologetic manner, 'All soldiers are good. We are people of peace with a misunderstanding.'

At dawn, all sympathy was put aside. Any misunderstanding was blown away with the mortars, rockets and heavy machine guns that pounded the

Burmese compound. From the trench, Ge Ge and two other gunners beside me took aim and fired at the confused Burmese soldiers who were rudely awakened. Bunkered down in the trench, my main concern was not the mortars and rockets flying overhead, but the lack of light available for taking pictures.

In order to get better shots, I began to stand up in the trench until another gunner, my friend Saw Ba Wah, urged me to keep down. As the battle raged and dawn turned into day, my lighting concerns vanished, allowing me to focus on getting better angles. It's amazing how looking through a viewfinder can disguise reality.

The onslaught continued for about an hour and a half before the guerrillas made their final push to the main compound at Tojo. Cheered on by yelling soldiers in the back, who provided them cover with mortars and heavy machine gun fire, two attack groups stormed the camp and successfully overran it after a fierce gunfight. I followed with Ba Wah and Ge Ge, expecting to find 30 dead Burmese on the hill, but instead found only one—the rest had fled. The dead man lay in a bunker with a bullet hole through his head.

'Bloody fool,' screamed Ba Wah as he unloaded three rounds of his AK-47 into the dead man's chest. 'This is what you get for trying to fight us!'

It was strange to see this man, so kind and gentle off the battlefield, behaving so callously on it. His wrath was not unfounded though, ten of his family members and more than 100 of his friends have died at the hands of the Burmese military. Facts like these tend to put matters into perspective.

While one group of Karen guerrillas pursued the fleeing Burmese soldiers into the jungle, the remaining searched the camp for supplies. Thousands of rounds of bullets were found along with rockets, mortar shells, and a few weapons. Besides military equipment, the Karen also took maps, notebooks and some personal artefacts including an un-mailed letter found in the bag of the dead soldier. It was a note to his sister pleading with her to take care of their mother. I kept the letter and later gave it to a Karen woman in Mae Sot, who read it with tears rolling down her face.

'It is not people who are bad,' she said, 'it is governments.' For the first time in her life, she later told me, she realized that Burmese soldiers are human beings just like Karen soldiers, who love their family and don't want to die.

Still, battlefields can bring out the darker side of people. While the guerrillas were raiding the camp for supplies, I saw another Karen man disembowel the dead Burmese soldier. The scene haunted me for days and left me questioning the nature of humanity, and how witnessing its dark side would affect me as a person. Walking down the mountain that day I even considered giving up on war zones. I felt sick inside; sick from the stench of battle, and sick from the grisly image of that young man carving up the dead man's chest.

But it only took a few days to recover (with the help of a five-star hotel in Bangkok and my Karen girlfriend), and I was soon back in the jungle with the KNLA, chasing the dragon of combat. In battle, life becomes centered around the moment and everything else becomes meaningless. There is no yesterday, no tomorrow, no past, no future; everything is crunched into the present and all other references in time and place have vanished. I have never felt more alive than in battle, or never more at peace than in its aftermath. And while battlefields can bring out our demons, they also can bring out our decency. After all, war is humanity's single largest producer of heroes.

A few months later, I witnessed such decency during an ambush when a 26-year-old KNLA guerrilla threw off his equipment and rushed back towards the enemy to save his wounded comrade who had been hit by a grenade. He returned a few minutes later with the wounded man on his back and carried him to safety in the forest where medics were able to treat him. The soldier, Ku Kwa, then helped carry his friend in a hammock that was tied to a bamboo pole. He helped carry him for several kilometers until the injured man insisted on walking on his own. With four body wounds, the man got out of the hammock and limped slowly through the jungle—at times crawling on his hands and knees. It was a display of both heroism and determination that any army in the world would have recognized with medals of valor and sacrifice. In the KNLA though, these soldiers were just doing their duty; a duty that for more than half a century has been willingly accepted by tens of thousands of Karen men who have taken up arms to fight for their homeland. It is one of the longest and least known conflicts in the world today, which pits one of the world's most repressive military regimes against one of the world's most feeble and ill-equipped guerrilla armies.

The conflict began on 31 January 1949, when soldiers of the Karen National Defence Organization (KNDO) opened fire on Burmese government troops advancing on their headquarters in the township of Insein, just north of the capital Rangoon. The Burmese troops were to enforce a government decree that outlawed the Karen militia, which had been formed in 1947. KNDO forces held the town, overran much of northern Burma, and some of their troops even advanced within seven kilometres of the capital, but agreed to a three-day ceasefire in early April.

'That was our first mistake,' a KNLA General would lament to me 58 years later. 'If we continued fighting, we would be the government today.'

There is a Karen folktale called the Tiger and the Man, which I read for the first time on one of many journeys inside Karen State, and all I could think about was how closely it related to the first days of the war between the Karen and the Burmese. It tells the story of a poor farmer who every morning would leave his breakfast in his hut before cultivating his field, and every morning would find it gone when be came back to eat it.

On realizing that a tiger was stealing it, he set a trap to catch him. Sure enough, the next morning when the farmer was in his field, he heard the roars of the tiger that had been caught in his trap. The man rushed to the scene and the tiger pleaded for the man to save him. He admitted responsibility for the theft but implored forgiveness, saying it was not a serious crime and that he had now been punished sufficiently by the trap. The man refused to help him for he feared the tiger would eat him on being released. The tiger solemnly swore to the man that he would not eat him and the man eventually gave in and released him.

But as soon as he was let out of the trap, the tiger seized the man and was about to devour him. The man pleaded to the tiger and reminded him of his oath not to eat him. The tiger told him necessity knew no law, and that since he was now crippled, he could no longer hunt for game; so he must either eat the farmer or starve. Just then, a hare happened to pass by and the case was referred to him for a decision. The wise hare said to them, 'Look, I can't understand this matter clearly. The both of you need to act out just what happened.'

And so they did and again the tiger entered the trap, but was careful to avoid the spring.

'I don't know how you can justly complain about what has happened to you,' said the hare to the tiger. 'How could you have received those terrible bruises?' The tiger, wanting to demonstrate the reason for the bruises, edged nearer and nearer until he touched the spring and the trap fell again. 'Attack him!' yelled the hare to the man. 'And never again restore an advantage to an enemy too strong for you.'

The ceasefire accepted by the KNDO in April 1949 did exactly what the hare warns the man never to do again: it restored an advantage to an enemy too strong for them. As the Karen's leader, Saw Ba U Gyi, went to Rangoon for peace negotiations, the battered Burma Army used the ceasefire to bring down reinforcements by plane from the north, landing at the airport in Insein, which had just been made safe from the lull in the fighting. With no concessions offered and the government demanding unconditional surrender, Saw Ba U Gyi left Rangoon in disgust. As soon as the ceasefire expired, government forces launched an offensive. KNDO forces were able to hold onto the town for several more weeks until making a tactical retreat under the cover of darkness in the early hours of 22 May 1949. Since then, tactical retreats have been a common feature of the Karen's war against the Burmese government.

Despite controlling much of Burma in 1949, the Karen had always lived in the political shadow of the Burmese. It is generally accepted that the Karen arrived in the region that is now modern-day Burma a few centuries before the Burmese. It is presumed they migrated south from Mongolia, through the Gobi desert and southern China, and then into Burma around the seventh century AD. The Karen, however, never organized themselves politically until the late 19th century. Once the Burmese arrived between the ninth and 11th centuries, the Karen were immediately treated as an inferior race and were subjugated through centuries of persecution and oppression. This forced many to move into the remote highlands of the east where they lived in relative isolation with limited contact beyond neighboring villages.

The Karen had no written language so their culture and history relied heavily on oral accounts of their myths, legends and folklore. One legend told of a lost white younger brother who would return one day with the lost Golden Book of the Karen. In 1828, the lost white brother with the Golden Book finally appeared in the form of Adoniram Judson, an American missionary. His first convert among the Karen was a slave, who immediately set out through the jungles to spread the Christian word to other Karen communities. Villagers were converted by the thousands in what has to be one of the greatest missionary success stories in history. A few years later, another American missionary began to invent a written script for the Sgaw Karen language (the Sgaw is one of numerous tribes that make up the Karen). Soon Christian missionary schools began springing up across the region, enabling a large number of Karen to receive a high level of education. The work of the missionaries ultimately gave rise to a Karen national identity that united them as a people. In a relatively short period of time, the Karen went from being a scattered band of hill tribes and villages with no sense of national identity or ethnic consciousness to being a proud, unified, and culturally distinct nation of peoples who were willing to defend this newfound identity with patriotic zeal.

Despite the success of the missionaries, Karen Christians never constituted more than 15 percent of the Karen population, with the remainder consisting of Buddhists or animists. Not surprisingly though, Karen

Christians set up and led the Karen's first political organization in 1881, the Karen National Association (KNA), and they have dominated their political and military movement ever since.

Missionary activity with the Karen in the 19th century coincided with the conquest and colonization of Burma by the British. The Karen welcomed the British with open arms and willingly fought alongside them against the Burmese—payback for nearly a thousand years of persecution and oppression. Thousands of Karen joined the colonial army and police force, and played major roles in maintaining order and in suppressing various Burmese rebellions. The Burmese, on the other hand, considered the British to be invaders of their kingdom and a threat to their Buddhist faith. The Karen, who viewed the British as protectors and saviours, would be loyal to them until the very end, an end that would ultimately see them betrayed and abandoned.

When World War Two broke out and Japanese forces invaded and took control of Burma, the Karen formed the backbone of the underground resistance while Burmese nationalists, under the banner of the newly formed Burma Independence Army (BIA), sided with the Japanese. The war not only pitted the Burmese and Karen against each other again, but it also created the opportunity for many of them to settle long-smouldering disputes by the use of force, especially for the Burmese nationalists to take revenge on the Karen for their cooperation with the British. In the first half of 1942, 1,800 Karen were killed and 400 villages were destroyed by the BIA in one district alone. In another district, Papun, located in the eastern hills,

17 Karen elders were taken hostage by the BIA and later executed, while another BIA rampage slaughtered 152 Karen civilians, including women and children. These massacres have never been forgotten.

The British remained in contact with the Karen throughout the war, with some British soldiers operating with them in the eastern hills. Over 12,000 weapons were airdropped by the British into Karen territory, and several officers and soldiers parachuted to join the resistance. The war further united the Karen as a people and also gave them the weapons, equipment, knowledge, and experience which would be vital for launching a resistance movement of their own. But before doing so, they would kill over 12,500 retreating Japanese troops as Allied Forces regained control of Burma in the final stages of the war.

The Karen trusted the British and believed they would help their cause. After the war, Karen leaders agreed to press the British for a separate Karen State— something that individual British officers had promised them throughout the war. Ultimately these promises meant very little but they were regarded by the Karen as official pledges coming directly from Westminster. Notwithstanding this, these promises have never been forgotten.

Karen leadership sent their request to London but it went unanswered. Following up on this, a Karen delegation travelled to London in August 1946 to push for either a Karen State operating under British protection, or for a Karen State in a Federation of Frontier Area States that were separate from Burma and in the British Commonwealth. They returned to

Burma empty-handed. Six months later, 700 delegates from all the existing Karen parties gathered in Rangoon for an All Karen Congress where they agreed to merge all their parties into one, the Karen National Union (KNU), which, to this day, remains the Karen's political arm. In one last desperate attempt before independence was granted to Burma in January 1948, the KNU sent British Prime Minister Clement Attlee a final plea for an independent Karen State. Over a century of undying loyalty was repaid only with silence and dismissal. The message was clear: the Karen were on their own. If the Karen wanted independence, they would have to fight for it. So that's what they did—and they are still fighting today.

In early January 2001, two months after the attack on Tojo, I embarked on another journey with the Karen. I would be gone for 59 days, tramping through an estimated 500 kilometers of some of the most inhospitable jungle in Burma, not knowing at the time of setting out exactly how formidable this journey was going to be.

I was laden with several kilos of gear including two stills cameras and a newly acquired video camera which was loaned to me by Jerry Harmer from the Bangkok office of *Associated Press Television News*. I soon found myself physically unprepared for the grueling trek across several mountains to reach the KNLA's ninth battalion headquarters—one of farthest KNLA battalions stationed inside Burma from the Thai border. My guide was a Karen man named Sheemoh, who spent the majority of his time in Mae Sot, but who would go 'inside' a couple of months a year in order to fight with the KNLA. He was fluent in English, well-spoken, and an expert in military tactics. He was even versed in Sun Tzu's 'Art of War' which he believed to be great in theory but not very practicable. His assessment of Sun Tzu was not an academic appraisal—he was speaking from direct experience. Sheemoh was also an excellent companion and a passionate fighter.

We crossed the Salween River from Thailand and reached the KNLA-held village of Ho Kay. Sheemoh and I waited for almost a week in a small hut before continuing on by boat to Mae Nu Tah and then again by foot into the Bu Tho mountain range. The first day of the trek was probably the most grueling day of my life. It started out with a two-hour steep ascent up the first mountain, before a long, steep descent into the valley below. It didn't take long for me to realize that my new boots were half a size too small—a painfully frustrating realization in the first hour of a major expedition into a remote war zone. The pain of the skin lesions that were oozing blood through my socks was soon overshadowed by the pain of physical exhaustion as we ascended the open slope of a second mountain in the blazing heat of the mid afternoon sun. I climbed the slope a few steps step at a time, collapsing several times in utter exhaustion, forcing myself to get back up and take just a few more steps, grasping for air and drowning in my own desperation; my legs and lungs screaming for me to stop. Somehow I willed myself to the top before one last descent to our day's destination, the small Karen village of Leh Thaw Ko. With no more than 100 meters to the house where we were to spend the night, I collapsed again in utter exhaustion on the slight ascent towards the house.

'Can I just sleep here?' I asked Sheemoh, honestly thinking I could not make it another 100 meters to the house.

'On the ground?' Sheemoh replied.

'Yes, you can go on ahead but I'll just sleep here, I don't mind.' Shaking his head in disbelief, he urged me to get up and walk the last 100 or so meters to the house. I don't know how, but I did. Once inside the house, I laid down on the hardboard floor in a state of euphoria, drifting in and out of sleep, wanting time to stand still so tomorrow would never come.

When I woke the next morning, I decided to ditch my boots to wear my Birkenstock sandals instead— not the ideal footwear for a jungle trek, but far more comfortable than my small-sized boots. I figured if the Karen could trek through the jungle in flip-flops, then my three-strap Birkenstocks should do just fine. I was wrong, but I wore them for the next couple of weeks before a KNLA commander picked me up a pair of Burmese jungle boots through underground connections in a nearby town. They set me back 800 Burmese Kyat, about a dollar.

It was easy to indulge in self-pity during the first couple of days of the journey, until I saw the realities of Karen State and the suffering of its people. While my pain was temporary, their pain was what they called life. I was there by choice; they were there by force. It's hard to feel sorry for yourself when you have it better than all of those around you. Self-pity has no place in a land of despair.

After four days of walking, Sheemoh and I—now accompanied by about a dozen KNLA soldiers—reached the command post of Sheemoh's cousin, Captain Gee Gi, the KNLA's Third Brigade Intelligence Officer (the KNLA has seven brigades, with three battalions making up each brigade. In addition, there are five special battalions making a total of 26. The ninth battalion, which was where Sheemoh and I were headed, is under the Third Brigade, the brigade responsible for Nyaunglebin district.)

Born near the township of Insein, Gee Gi was three and a half years old when the war began in 1949, and lived a relatively privileged life until he decided to join the resistance in 1972.

'There have been two parts of my life,' he later explained to me. 'I attended school; then I attended the revolution.' When I asked him why he decided to join the revolution, he answered simply, 'Because I love my people.'

A few kilometers from Gee Gi's command post in Gher Pha tract, Papun district, alongside a picturesque shore of the Bellin River, 70 Karen families were living a meager existence in a makeshift forest camp. They had fled their villages the previous November after the Burmese army had launched an operation to wrest the area from KNLA control.

'Many villages were destroyed,' Gee Gi explained. He took out a map and pointed to five villages,

'Pawwahdo, destroyed; Mawpu, destroyed; Perkhido, destroyed; Thikapawdo, destroyed; Yohpolaw, destroyed ...' Most of the villagers were able to flee in time, but not all. The 365th, 367th and 369th Infantry Battalions of the Burmese army had done their jobs well.

Naw Tah Reeh Poh, a 60-year-old grandmother, lost her daughter in the attack—she was shot dead by Burmese soldiers. I met her in the camp along the Bellin River holding a tiny baby in her arms. The baby was her granddaughter, whom she now had to care for, barely keeping her alive by feeding her sweetened water. Despite the cruelty inflicted on her family, she told me her heart was full of forgiveness, perhaps a result of her Christian faith as she approached her final days on earth.

'My life has been a hard life,' she told me with an empty stare as if all the life had been drained out of her, 'but I don't want to blame Burmese soldiers—I have forgiveness.' In a grandmother's summary of the situation, she simply said, 'The Burmese didn't want us anymore, so they came to our village to persecute us.'

The destruction of villages and the forced relocation of their inhabitants has been a tactic used by the Burmese army since the late 1960s as part of its Four Cuts counter-insurgency strategy. Modeled on British and American counter-insurgency programs, the Four Cuts policy seeks to cut the four main links between insurgents, their families and local villagers. These are food, funds, intelligence, and recruits. Gee Gi adds one more, 'our heads'. The idea is to cut the rebels' civilian support base—'to drain the sea in order to kill the fish,' as a Burmese proverb goes. By implementing this policy, the Burmese army has purposely targeted the civilian populations located in rebel areas. In the words of Gee Gi, 'the Burmese army clears Karen villages with bullets'.

Since 1996, it is estimated that over three thousand villages in Eastern Burma have been destroyed, relocated or abandoned as a result of the Four Cuts policy. One such village was Tahreeta, home to about 30 people, located approximately 15 kilometers from the Salween River in Papun district in the KNLA's Fifth Brigade area. In February 2002, I witnessed its destruction. I was with a company of KNLA soldiers who were patrolling the area when we approached the scene, arriving about an hour after Burmese soldiers had set it ablaze. The last of the flames were still burning when we arrived at the scene, the village reduced to smouldering ashes, scorched earth and a few skeletal remains of what used to be homes. According to Sheemoh, the soldiers destroyed it because they were angered by a recent clash with the rebels who injured one of their men and also because they believed the village was supporting the KNLA. They were right. And one of the reasons why the inhabitants of Tahreeta supported the rebels was because the rebels didn't burn down their homes.

I stood among angry soldiers in the ashes; their faces screamed of sadness and of vengeance as they clutched their weapons, staring at the ruins. A few days before, Sheemoh had told me about a Karen proverb that says they will rule over their land when the worms eat all of the soil. 'I'm not sure what it means,' he told me, 'but I think it means we will rule our land when we have nothing left of it.' Now, they were one less village closer.

Luckily, the inhabitants of Tahreeta had fled their village before the Burmese arrived and all of them escaped with their lives. This is typically the case in areas where the KNLA is prevalent. Villagers are forewarned by the rebels of Burmese operations and will flee their villages ahead of time, leaving them as internally displaced people (IDPs) hiding in the jungle. At any given time, it is estimated that there are about 85,000 civilians hiding or living in temporary settlements in Burma as a result of the Four Cuts policy. When this number is added with those who are living in temporary relocation sites in non-conflict areas and those who have been moved to relocation sites by government troops, the number jumps to well over half a million—one of the highest IDP rates in the world.

In the IDP camp along the Bellin River, people were going about their daily lives as best as they could. Most of their time was spent preparing for their next meal. They would forage the forest for food, fish, prepare rice, collect firewood, and cook over open fires. These forgotten people lived in makeshift bamboo shelters spread out across the riverbank; a grim existence but nothing they weren't accustomed to. Although this was my first encounter with an IDP camp, I would soon become quite familiar with them as I crisscrossed areas of Karen State over the next few years. I once encountered dozens of villagers in the forest on the move, having just fled their homes in the wake of an imminent Burmese operation—and they were laughing and smiling! Their village was about to be destroyed; they were homeless, on the run, and were lacking in both food and medicine. They were hiding in the forest because their government wanted to kill them, and yet they were laughing and smiling; the profoundest misery surmounted by an unbreakable spirit. Back in their village, they had a home and probably a few farm animals—not much, but now they didn't even have that. Instead of crying, they were shaking my hand saying 'thank you.' They were thanking me because I had journeyed into Karen State to witness and document their plight. And as I photographed and shot video footage of them in order to portray their suffering, all I could think of was, 'please stop smiling.' They weren't supposed to be smiling.

In Gher Pha tract, Sheemoh and I stayed with Captain Gee Gi and his family for a few days before continuing on our journey towards the ninth battalion. Gee Gi spoke excellent English, and he and I would stay up late into the night conversing beside the campfire. He told me harrowing stories, like how two of his nieces, aged two and three, were killed in their village four years before.

'Burmese troops attacked the village and began firing at the villagers. The people began to run for their lives. Two Burmese soldiers grabbed my nieces and threw them into a burning house. They were burned alive.'

In another Burmese operation, Gee Gi told me about a month when 70 Karen villagers were killed to rid the area of KNLA insurgents.

'They killed one man, decapitated him, and put his head on the road with a cigarette in his mouth to scare the other villagers. That month, 70 villagers were found dead floating in the nearby river.

'Not a good nation, the Burmese nation,' he said, while Sheemoh added, 'I cannot forgive them like the grandma.'

It had been more than two weeks since crossing the Salween River into Karen State when Sheemoh and I finally arrived in the village of Ler Wah, the headquarters of the KNLA's ninth battalion. The village was home to no more than a hundred people, mostly KNLA soldiers and their family members. According to Sheemoh, I was the first journalist ever to visit the area.

Once there, I was introduced to Second-Lieutenant Myint Oo, a platoon commander of the battalion's second company. Unusually tall and well built for a Karen, he was a natural leader who embodied the stereotypical qualities of a warrior. Since most of his senior officers were outside of Ler Wah, he was one of the highest ranking soldiers in the area and ensured that I was well taken care of over the next several weeks.

With a column of Burmese soldiers lurking somewhere in the nearby jungle, and two battalions of the Burmese infantry preparing for an offensive in the area, I set out with the ninth battalion's second company after six days in Ler Wah on an operation to ambush their enemy. Aware that the weight of my bag could prove a life-threatening burden if I wasn't able to keep up with the company in enemy territory, Sheemoh kindly asked around for someone to help carry some of my equipment. One soldier immediately volunteered. His name was Tee Poh, a soft-spoken, kind-hearted guerrilla only slightly younger than me in his early 20s. Not only did he help carry some of my equipment, he also took it upon himself to look after me and assist me in every way he could. He was truly a kind person who would have taken a bullet for me. Over the next few weeks, he rarely left my side and even guided me back to Thailand at the end of my journey. He ended up assisting me on two other trips into Karen State over the next two years, becoming one of my most loyal friends formed in the Karen jungle.

After a two-day walk to reach the estimated vicinity of the Burmese column, the company spent the next week or so of the operation gathering intelligence by listening to enemy radio transmissions and sending out scout teams to look for signs of the enemy. Apart from the first night spent in a Karen village, we were living in the jungle in makeshift camps, usually moving every day or two depending on the situation. I was amazed by how fast the soldiers could set up a camp; in a matter of minutes they could turn a small piece of jungle into a habitable settlement. Small trees and brush would be cleared with machetes, pathways would be made, hammocks would be tied to trees, firewood would be gathered and water collected from nearby streams, and—most impressive of all for me—utensils, such as spatulas for cooking, would be carved out of bamboo. Tee Poh was a master at this and took great pride in his work, always ensuring the end result was a smooth, well-shaped and even-sided spatula. 'For God's sake, Tee Poh,' I would think to myself. 'It's just a spatula!'

Food was scarce, and some days we had nothing to eat except rice. I soon learned that adding chillies and cooking oil to a plain bowl of rice is actually not a bad meal. This was an accidental discovery as Tee Poh, embarrassed that they only had plain rice for me to eat, handed me a bottle of a clear liquid which I immediately thought was rice wine. Excitedly, I put the bottle to my mouth and took a big gulp only to realize it was actually cooking oil. Needless to say, it tasted much better on the rice.

At night, some of the guerrillas would go hunting for wild cat (called *Tawanar* in Karen). They would shine their flashlights up and down the trees to try and freeze them in the light, while perched on a branch. Stunned and motionless, the cat became an easy target for their assault rifles. The animal, not much bigger than a domesticated cat, became a regular meal over the next few weeks, and provided us with one of our main sources of protein.

On day five of the operation—by now I had been in Karen State for one month—Myint Oo asked me if I would like to buy anything from the nearby Burmese town of Kyauk Kyi. He had connections in the town and could arrange for goods to be brought to us. Sometimes he would even go himself—changing out of his military uniform and into a traditional Burmese sarong-like male skirt called a *longyi* and a t-shirt. He also packed a pistol in his *longyi*—for emergency use only. Excitedly, I gave him the equivalent of about $30 and asked him to get beef and beer. The next evening, after setting up our fourth camp in five days, we enjoyed a jungle feast which was served with a dozen bottles of warm Mandalay Beer. Beer never tasted so good. Since the town itself was only a few kilometers away, and since our present location marked the beginning of the Burmese lowlands and the edge of the Karen's jungle, I basked in the proud realization that I had walked all the way across Karen State. I lay down in my hammock that night and for the first time in weeks fell asleep satisfied and in a wonderful alcoholic buzz. I've always wondered if the Burmese army ever came across that empty campsite, and what they would have made of all those empty beer bottles. Surely it would not have been good for their morale.

Around this time, a Karen man from a village near Kyauk Kyi came to our jungle camp to talk with the rebels and provide information. Like the majority of Karen in the area, he was sympathetic to the rebels, even though he lived in a village under government control. He explained to me that his village had to provide two porters for the Burmese army and three people for forced labor at all times, based on a rotating system in the village. The military also forced the villagers to regularly provide supplies such as food without any compensation. In addition, every morning at 7am, a designated person from the village had to report to the military command at Kyauk Kyi on the security situation in and around their village, especially pertaining to KNLA activity. He then explained that if the military command received relevant information that went unreported, then the village headman would be executed. When I asked him what would happen to him if the military found out that he had come to visit us, he replied that his minimum punishment would be a very long prison sentence. 'But probably I'd be executed', he said. I admired his bravery.

As this Karen villager indicted, the use of forced labor in Burma is widespread. The military junta, known as the State Peace and Development Council (SPDC), forces an estimated 800,000 people a year to work for little or no pay. Civilians who refuse are threatened with imprisonment, while laborers who do not carry out their tasks properly are beaten or killed. In ethnic conflict areas such as Karen State, forced labor is even more prevalent, with civilians forced to carry out numerous duties for the military, of which being a porter is the most common.

On my many journeys into Karen State, I have met two different groups of porters who had just reached KNLA positions after being forced to carry supplies for the Burmese army. The first group consisted of two Karen men who had just been relieved of their duties and were heading back home through KNLA lines. I met them in February 2002 in a jungle camp in the KNLA's Fifth Brigade area, about 15 kilometers from the Thai border. They told me government troops, who were on an offensive in the area, had raided their village eight days before, looting it for food and supplies, and forcing many of its people to act as porters for the next eight days. They said they were treated very badly, forced to carry an extremely heavy load and were often beaten. They also acted as human minesweepers, being forced to walk in front of the troops to be the first to detonate any landmines, another common practice of the Burmese military.

While these two men performed their duty without injury, another porter in the operation was not as lucky. As a human minesweeper, he met the fate of his job's worst fear. That evening, he was brought into the KNLA camp where I was staying. He was carried in a hammock tied to a bamboo pole with half his foot missing. The next day, in a make-shift jungle clinic nearby, Karen medics amputated his leg just below the knee, performing a near-flawless surgery that few doctors in the world could have performed with such limited resources. When I showed the video I took of the operation to a Norwegian doctor in Mae Sot six years later, he watched it with tears in his eyes. He had personally trained some of the medics in the video and for the first time he was able to see them performing a real surgery. He was unbelievably impressed and proud of his former students performing an almost flawless surgery.

In October 2003, I met another group of porters at the KNLA's Seventh Brigade headquarters of Ta Kaw Bee Tah. The group consisted of 11 Burmese men who had just escaped from their army captors after more than a month of portering for them. They had arrived after walking for four days through the jungle in order to reach KNLA lines. Oddly, they had all been taken from jails in Burma and been forced to carry ammunition and supplies for a massive government offensive. About 1,000 porters were being used for this particular operation, which was launched in August

2003 and included ten battalions of the Burmese army.

One of the men, Zaw Win, aged 46, said that for more than a month he was forced to carry 2,000 rounds of ammunition which weighed about 25 kilograms. He had been taken from a prison in Bago division of Central Burma where he was jailed for involvement in an underground lottery.

'All the porters are afraid,' he told me. 'They want to run away but they are afraid of landmines and they don't know the way.' He also said that when the porters are walking with Burmese soldiers, they must keep pace or they are punished. 'You cannot rest. If you do they will kick you or hit you with a stick,' he said.

All 11 men were underweight, having been fed only once a day as porters and then eating nothing at all during their four-day ordeal in trying to reach rebel lines. Many of them had badly cut shoulders from carrying supplies on their backs in bamboo baskets. Win said the porters had been told by their captors that if they escaped and managed to reach KNLA positions, the rebels would cut off their heads. But it wasn't the rebels he was afraid of. 'I'm just afraid of the SPDC,' he told me.

Not only does the Burmese army impose forced labor on civilians, but it also engages in the forced conscription of recruits, often targeting children. As a result, Burma is believed to have the highest number of child soldiers in the world, with rights groups such as Human Rights Watch estimating that there are over 70,000 soldiers under the age of 18 in the Burmese army—accounting for 20 percent of the world's total.

The army commonly captures boys around the age of 15, usually in public places such as train and bus stations, markets and movie theatres, giving them two choices: join the army, or go to jail. They are often brutalized by their commanders, forced to carry out human rights abuses, and typically not allowed to go on leave during the first five years of their service.

Twice I have met such recruits who had recently deserted their units and fled to KNLA positions. The first time was at Ner Dah's Walaykey base in October 2002. The deserter's name was Ton Ton U and he was 17 years old, having been in the army since he was 14. He told me military men had taken him from a movie theatre in his hometown of Pyay and forced him to the join the army. 'They told me if I refused to join, they would put me in jail.' He soon wound up in Karen State fighting the KNLA, but he had no idea what the war was about. He said he was treated very badly in the army and was beaten for the smallest of mistakes. After three years, he took his chances with the rebels he had never met, as well as the landmines that lay in the way, left his sentry while on duty, and just started to walk. Nine hours later he saw a Karen soldier, surrendered and gave his weapon to him, and asked to be taken to the nearest KNLA camp. After several days of questioning, KNLA leaders let him go to Thailand where he has remained ever since.

In March 2003, I met two more Burmese child soldiers who had recently deserted to the KNLA. Nay Myo Kyaw, aged 16, and Aung Myoo Oo, aged 15, had just fled their units at Tojo and were picked up by Karen soldiers and brought to Walaykey. Before his kidnap, Kyaw was a ninth grade student in the southeastern Burmese town of Thongwa. He told me that he was walking home from school with friends one day the previous October when a car pulled up alongside them. Military men got out of the car and forced him and his four schoolmates inside. Without a chance to say goodbye to their families, Kyaw and his four friends were conscripted into the Burmese army.

Kyaw was given only a month of military training before being sent to Tojo to fight against the KNLA. He quickly found out that he had no skills to deal with either the jungle or the war. Emotionless, he told me how he was punished by his officer in charge when he could not handle the heavy loads he was expected to carry. 'He beat me, slapped me, kicked me and whipped me with a stick.'

Of the 150 soldiers in his battalion, 70 of them were under the age of 17—and the youngest was only 11. After four months at Tojo and fearing for his life, Kyaw decided to put his fate in the hands of the soldiers against whom he was forced to fight. One day while on security duty, he simply dropped his rifle and equipment and started to run. 'I knew if I stayed there I would die,' he told me. He was picked up by Karen soldiers a few hours later.

In six months, Kyaw had gone from being a schoolboy to a child soldier, and finally a deserter in a rebel camp. He was tough as nails, but still a child. 'I just want to go home and see my mother and father,' he told me.

While the KNLA also has children within its ranks, there is a fundamental difference between child soldiers in the Burmese army and those in the KNLA: in the KNLA they are there by choice. I have never met a child soldier in the KNLA who did not wish to be there, while one 12-year-old I met continuously begged his commander to allow him to participate in combat operations. His name was Maung Loke Sar (meaning 'Work and Eat' in English) and I met him in the KNLA's Fifth Brigade area in February 2002. His father was dead and his mother sent him to live with a monk when he was just five years old. That was the last time he saw her. For three years he followed the monk until one day the man disappeared. He was left abandoned in a KNLA-controlled village where he was essentially adopted by the rebels. He wasn't allowed to become a soldier at such a young age, so the KNLA eventually sent him to attend school in the village of Day Bu Noh where I first met him in January 2001 as an 11-year-old schoolboy. The next time I saw him, just over a year later, he was wearing a uniform, a Rambo-like bandana around his head and carrying an M-16. Apparently, school was not for him.

He was assigned to a KNLA unit in the Fifth Brigade where he acted as an aid to the area's strategy commander, performing menial duties such as cooking and washing. He wasn't happy with such tasks and continuously pleaded with his commander to allow him to go on frontline operations. 'I'm a man,' he would tell him, 'I can fight.' But his commander always said no.

I met him several times in February 2002 in the Fifth Brigade area. What struck me most about him was his constant cheerfulness and willingness to perform his duties as a soldier. The KNLA gave him a sense of belonging; it was his family. He was truly one of the happiest and most passionate soldiers I have ever met. He was also tough. The last time I saw him he was giving himself a tattoo, lacerating his arm with a needle dipped in ink. 'I would never do that,' Sheemoh commented.

The day after our jungle feast of beef and beer near the Burmese town of Kyauk Kyi, Myint Oo and his men discovered a newly made trail on the mountain just a few kilometers away. Close inspection of the trail revealed that its makers were walking up the mountain, and no other trail was found leading down. For the rebels, it was a clear indication that the column of Burmese soldiers they knew to be in the vicinity were somewhere up the mountain nearby, but there was a problem. Radio intercepts were actually indicating the opposite—that the column was somewhere at the bottom of the mountain.

Confused and cautious, the rebels spent the next few days trying to gather better intelligence on their enemy's location. Radio signals and transmissions were being monitored almost continuously by the company's radio interceptor, whose job it was to listen in on SPDC transmissions using a radio receiver, to decipher codes, and to analyze the information deciphered. Meanwhile, two and three-man recon teams were combing the surrounding area for signs of enemy activity. Finally, the rebels concluded that the column of Burmese soldiers were most likely on the mountain, so a trap was set to bring them down and lure them into an ambush.

Being outnumbered and outgunned, the KNLA never want to engage the SPDC in prolonged combat, instead relying on common guerrilla tactics such as raids and ambushes, characterized by surprise, shock, lethal force and rapid withdrawal. Ambushes are not only effective for offensive purposes, to harass the enemy and capture their weapons, but they are also effective for defensive purposes as they can divert and stall enemy operations.

A typical KNLA ambush is conducted by 15 to 40 soldiers and is usually initiated by at least one Claymore mine—a directional fragmentation landmine that fires shrapnel out to about 100 meters. The rebels set up position along a route they believe the enemy will pass through, usually setting up under the cover of darkness and concealing their positions behind jungle growth. In the event that the enemy comes, the guerrillas will initiate the ambush by detonating the Claymore(s), spraying the 'kill zone' with thousands of metal fragments, before unleashing their firepower.

For this particular ambush attempt, a small decoy team was sent down the mountain to walk along a Burmese-controlled road just outside Kyauk Kyi. This was done in order to show that there was a KNLA presence in the area. This would hopefully lure the SPDC column down the mountain to engage the unit, and thence straight into an ambush. The ambush itself was set up by the rest of the company along the most likely route that the column would take. Just before dusk, we set out from our jungle camp to the designated ambush position along a dirt road—the first road I had seen in over a month—and spent a restless night a few hundred meters away from it, concealed in the bushes, before moving into position just before dawn. Then we began to wait.

Waiting in an ambush is a surreal experience, a rare time when all your senses are focused on your immediate surroundings, a small particle of time and space into which your whole life seems to be compressed. Adrenaline and anticipation pump through your body, readying it for action, but all you can do is just sit and wait, staring into the abyss from which the enemy will emerge, hoping for the best. And as time goes by, seconds turn into minutes, and minutes into hours, you start thinking that the enemy isn't coming; you become anxious and restless; you stand up and take a piss; you begin to fade and test your luck, throwing your lot with the rebels beside you hoping that fate will get you through.

This particular ambush was my first with the KNLA but I would go on another six over the next two years (three of which would be in the following 12 days), becoming a familiar experience that never lost its seductive strangeness. It's an exhilarating rush sitting in an ambush, facing imminent danger and staring down your fears. It gives you an entirely new appreciation for your life, how you view it, how you treat it, and how you live it. But the waiting game can be unbearable: it can quickly lead into a long, slow descent into a dangerous boredom that messes with your mind, turning common sense into a brewing ground of doubt.

On this particular day, the Burmese column did not fall for the trap. After about eight hours of waiting, the rebels left the roadside and retreated into the jungle. 'We challenged the enemy,' Sheemoh told me, 'but they are being careful. This is the art of war.'

A second ambush attempt was set up the next day along another route, but again the Burmese column did not come down the mountain. 'We have to be patient,' Sheemoh explained, for he must have sensed my edginess after waiting in ambush positions for two straight days. 'This is like a giant game of hide and seek, only not the kind that children play.'

The next day, the company found another newly-made trail leading up the mountain, indicating that the column most likely came down the mountain and then returned, perhaps cautious of a KNLA ambush. Whatever the case, another ambush attempt was set up the next morning in the belief that the column would again come down the mountain.

Again, the wait was unbearable. For the first hour or so, everyone was in position, concealed behind trees or bushes, maintaining their ambush rule of silence. But as time ticked by and there was no sign of the Burmese column, discipline started to slide, including mine. By 12:30pm the guerrilla in charge of detonating the Claymore was asleep. Other soldiers had moved out of their cover into more comfortable but vulnerable positions. Some of them were even talking to each other and many stood up to stretch their legs. None were maintaining the same discipline as during the first hour of the wait. It was probably a good thing that once again the column did not come.

In the late afternoon, we left the area and returned to the previous night's jungle camp a few kilometers up the mountain. Along the way, some of the soldiers picked a few wild plants to cook for dinner, a meager side dish for their meager meal. Indeed, most of the Karen's guerrilla life is not spent fighting, but in searching for food and preparing meals. The fight against the Burmese is only half the battle; they also have to fight for the simplest of amenities to ensure their survival in the jungle. Even when they are out on a combat operation, they will stop to hunt down an animal if they see one. Fish are caught in nearby streams using bamboo spears and homemade nets; fruits and nuts are picked from trees that they climb with ease; I've even seen them catch a mouse by luring it into a pile of leaves and then setting it ablaze. The jungle is their home, their provider, and the territory that they defend with their lives.

'I love the forest,' a KNLA soldier once told me as the monsoon rains pounded down on us, leaving us wet, cold and miserable, 'because it is here where I can fight so that one day I can have a home.'

After failing to lure the SPDC column into an ambush, despite three attempts in four days, Myint Oo was getting truly annoyed.

'The enemy is being very careful,' he told me, shaking his head in disappointment, as if he had been cheated out of something he was entitled to. 'We will have to wait for a better time.'

Three days later, he brought nine of his men within striking distance of a Burmese battalion outpost— Infantry Battalion 60—two kilometers northeast of Kyauk Kyi, and got two of his men to spray automatic weapons fire while he fired three rounds from his rocket-propelled grenade launcher. I could tell he was pleased to vent some of the frustration and rage that had been brewing over the past few days. That evening, after remaking an old camp for the night, the rebels celebrated their harassment of the enemy with a cheap bottle of rum bought from underground connections in Kyauk Kyi. We took turns taking shots, and for the second time in two weeks, I laid down in my hammock with a wonderful buzz.

Over the next few days, Myint Oo and his men devised one last ambush plan before returning to headquarters. Intelligence revealed that also camped on the mountain was a unit of the Democratic Karen Buddhist Army (DKBA), a factionalist group of the Karen that split away from the Christian-dominated KNLA in 1994 and subsequently allied itself with the government. It was a huge blow to the Karen's struggle, one in which they have never recovered from.

Not only did the split turn the Karen against themselves, but it also led to the immediate loss of the KNLA's stronghold of Manerplaw in January 1995. With hundreds of troops from the Buddhist breakaway faction acting as guides, government forces easily moved in on the area and captured the headquarters on 27 January 1995. On arriving, however, they found it deserted and burned to the ground, the last remaining defenders having destroyed it before fleeing across the border to Thailand.

Manerplaw, meaning 'Victory Field', had been the KNLA's headquarters since 1975. Located on the banks of the Moei River just opposite Thailand, its location summed up the status of the Karen's struggle better than any casualty list or war chart could. After decades of fighting, the Karen had been pushed from their original headquarters at Insein, 12 kilometers north of the capital, all the way east to the Thai border.

But things weren't *that* bad. Surrounded by steep, rugged mountains and Thailand to the east, Manerplaw was virtually impregnable and soon became a bustling center of resistance activity. It became the base of the National Democratic Front (NDF), an alliance of non-communist ethnic resistance groups set up in 1976 with Karen strongman Saw Bo Mya as its chairman, and later the base of Burma's pro-democratic opposition including the National League for Democracy (NLD), the Democratic Party for a New Society (DPNS) and a number of other smaller groups.

By 1976, Bo Mya had emerged as the most powerful leader in the Karen's struggle, holding the top positions in both the KNLA and its political wing, the KNU. Born in 1927 in Papun district, Bo Mya began his career as an anti-Japanese resistance fighter during World War Two. He joined the Karen's armed struggle at the onset and quickly made his way up the ranks, becoming a zone commander and attaining the rank of colonel by 1960. Over the next decade, he and a band of loyal and politically conservative officers assumed control of the Karen's insurgency and turned the remote, rugged hills of eastern Burma into an insurgent's haven known as the Karen rebel state of Kowthoolei. Controlling strategic trade routes along the Thai border, the rebels established a series of 'toll gates' which provided them with their most significant source of income. Through close links with the Thai military, weapons and ammunition were easily bought and smuggled across the border. Kowthoolei became the largest liberated zone in Burma.

Like most of the Karen's leadership and commissioned officers, Bo Mya was a Christian, having converted from animism in 1961. However, the majority of rank and file Karen soldiers since 1949 had been Buddhists. The Buddhist soldiers were recruited from the poorer villages and they lacked the education of many of the Christians. Therefore, they had always been at the lower end of the Karen's power base and had little opportunity to advance into leadership positions. Over the years, resentment began to grow as the predominantly Buddhist foot soldiers took the brunt of the fighting with little financial or political reward, while their Christian leaders lived comparatively comfortable lives in places like Manerplaw.

In 1989, a revered, Karen Buddhist monk named U Thuzana began constructing a pagoda in the village of Thu Mweh Hta, a few kilometers from Manerplaw, which soon became a source of fateful tension between Buddhists and Christians in the KNLA. The KNU had initially given permission for the pagoda's construction but this was later withdrawn since its white color and prominent position on the mountaintop made it too easy a target for which the Burmese army could use to direct artillery and air strikes against Manerplaw. Despite this however, U Thuzana ignored the order to stop construction, and an entire community was soon built up around the site, which became a popular Buddhist retreat. Followers received major privileges from government forces, such as exemption from forced labor and conscription, and could travel freely through the surrounding area without harassment from Burmese soldiers—or the KNLA. Many of the villagers began to believe that U Thuzana had magical, God-like powers, but in reality he just had a deal with the devil.

Supported and encouraged by the military regime, which was then known as the State Law and Order Restoration Council (SLORC), U Thuzana urged his followers to rise up against the KNLA. Hundreds rallied to his cause. After months of turmoil and failed negotiations, U Thuzana formed the Democratic Karen Buddhist Organization (DKBO) on 21 December 1994, and days later the armed wing of the faction, the DKBA. With promises that it would withdraw its troops from Karen State and give power to the DKBA, SLORC supplied the newly formed army and immediately used it to capture Manerplaw. With some 400 DKBA troops as guides (defectors from the KNLA who knew the area intimately), 10,000 government troops marched towards the KNLA headquarters and broke through the rebels' weakened defenses. Knowing they stood little chance of successfully defending the camp, the KNLA fought using delaying tactics before torching the place and making yet another tactical retreat. While the rebels only lost about ten soldiers, the loss of Manerplaw, which was the very symbol of their struggle, was devastating.

Within weeks of helping government forces to capture Manerplaw, the DKBA began attacking and burning Karen refugee camps in Thailand, viewing them as a support base for the KNLA and hoping to force the refugees back to Burma. Government forces not only encouraged this, but also accompanied the DKBA on such raids—something they had always wanted to do in the past but didn't want to risk damaging their relations with Thailand for blatant attacks on its soil. Rangoon could now blame rival Karen factions for such attacks. Over the next few years, hundreds of cross border attacks were launched by DKBA and government forces, but the violent attempt at intimidation didn't work: the refugees still believed they would be safer in Thailand than Burma. If anything, the attacks just gave them more reason to stay.

Viewed primarily as a government-supported militia, the DKBA never gained much support from the Karen population. Indeed, most of the original soldiers who had defected from the KNLA to form the DKBA in 1994 soon left. Most new soldiers joined for opportunist reasons or for such perks as having their family members exempted from forced labor. Others are forcibly recruited, while some are KNLA soldiers captured while on leave to visit family members and given two choices: either join us or die. No one joins or defects to the DKBA for dreams of an independent Karen homeland, and many defectors from the KNLA simply defect because they have family members living in DKBA-controlled areas.

Fielding a force of between 1,500 to 2,500 troops, the DKBA often fights against the KNLA in conjunction with the Burmese army, usually serving as guides or as small units attached to SPDC battalions. It engages in similar human rights abuses as the SPDC including the extortion of money and goods from villagers, forced labor, and violent intimidation. In effect, the DKBA is little more than a private army commanded by local warlords, lacking any clear political objective or honorable cause. The monopoly on Karen independence and honor belongs solely to the KNLA.

Back on the mountain near Kyauk Kyi, with a camp of DKBA soldiers pinpointed by the KNLA, the company was separated into three groups. The first group would attack the DKBA camp, which was believed to be holding eight soldiers and located about two kilometers up the mountain. The attack should trigger DKBA and SPDC reinforcements to come from nearby positions—and directly into the KNLA ambushes set up by the second and third groups along two different routes. I was instructed to go with group number two, led by Myint Oo.

On Day 22 of the operation since leaving the headquarters of Ler Wah, we set out down the mountain under cover of darkness towards the designated ambush site at the side of a dirt road. Unable to light a fire due to the proximity of our position to government forces and civilians who were required to report on KNLA activity, we spent a cold, restless night bunkered on the ground, fully dressed and combat-ready. Our only source of water was a nearby puddle. With my sleeping bag in another guerrilla's pack in a different group and the temperature falling to around 12 degrees, I pulled out an emergency blanket from my survival kit. It was a long, cold night waiting for the dawn.

At 4:30am the guerrillas took up their ambush positions. Two Claymore mines were set up about ten meters from the road and about 15 meters apart. The guerrillas in charge of detonating the Claymores concealed themselves about ten meters behind them. They were instructed to set them off at the same time, using a plastic trigger and ten meters of detonating cord as soon as the enemy entered the kill zone. The mines were concealed behind some brush, out of sight from the road. The 15 guerrillas of the ambush group were spread out in a horizontal formation about 20 meters parallel to the road, with the Claymores set up at the front end. The first Claymore had an improvised detonating device using a D-sized battery, while the second Claymore had a manufactured detonating 'clicker'.

Due to his position as the first man in the ambush, the guerrilla in charge of detonating the first Claymore also had to keep watch for the enemy and then give a thumbs-down signal to the man on his left to indicate the enemy's approach. This man would then signal to the next man, and so on down the formation.

The terrain was flat and both sides of the road led into dense forest, which provided the soldiers with an excellent escape route. It also provided the enemy with excellent cover to flee. In the darkness before first light, I set up position beside Tee Poh at the left end of the formation. My cameras were on the ground beside me, ready for action; while Tee Poh clutched his M-16, which was locked and loaded, safety off.

Tired from a sleepless night, half expecting that yet again the KNLA's enemy would not come, and not wanting to consciously go through another unbearable wait, I decided to close my eyes and allow myself to fall asleep. I was out cold, not the recommended state to be in when waiting in an ambush.

My morning started with a bang as I was violently awoken a couple of hours later by the earth-shattering sound of the Claymore. Instinctively, I grabbed my video camera and turned it on to film Tee Poh unleashing his firepower beside me. It all happened so fast. I awoke to complete chaos. Only the improvised Claymore had detonated because the guerrilla in charge of the second one was unfamiliar with its technology. There was bitter confusion amidst the bursts of gunfire, the explosions of grenades, the yelling and screaming, and frantic actions of battlefield rage. Within seconds of filming the fighting, something happened that has given me nightmares ever since: my battery died. Fuming like the guerrillas I was filming, I switched to my stills camera, snapped a shot of two KNLA guerrillas storming the road, and then frantically changed my battery to start filming again. And then there was silence; an eerie silence which deafened my ears more than any round of fire. I followed Myint Oo to the other side of the road, not knowing what was going on. I soon realized that the soldiers who had walked into the ambush had fled into the forest on the opposite side of the road. Suddenly Myint Oo hit the ground. I followed as the sound of an incoming M-79 grenade screamed towards us, shattering the silence.

'Retreat!' screamed Myint Oo. We ran off the road and back into the forest as the enemy launched a counter-attack. Three of the guerrillas couldn't run though due to the M-79 grenade fragments embedded in their bodies.

It was during the madness of the next few minutes that Ku Kwa stopped running, threw off his equipment and valiantly ran back towards the road to save his comrade, Thoo Lay, who had been hit by four grenade fragments in his legs, back and chest and was the only one of the wounded who couldn't walk on his own. Unarmed, Ku Kwa returned with him on his back, running until he was out of enemy range. The rest of the group stopped to quickly treat Thoo Lay along with the other two guerrillas—Zaw Naing, who was hit in both his legs, and Pa Gaw Koh, who took a fragment in his neck. A bamboo tree was cut down in seconds and a hammock was tied to it to make a stretcher for Thoo Lay; the other two would have to walk.

With incoming mortar fire to deal with, we began the climb up the mountain towards a jungle camp a few hours away. After the initial ascent up the mountain, Thoo Lay insisted on continuing on his own. Wrapped in bandages and heavily drugged on painkillers, he got out of the hammock and began to limp slowly and awkwardly up the jungle mountain, at times crawling on his hands and knees. It was an awesome display of raw determination; and if determination could kill an enemy like bullets, than the Burmese army and DKBA would have been slaughtered that day.

According to radio intercepts over the next day, three DKBA soldiers were badly wounded in the ambush and then died. The second KNLA ambush team hit a combine column of SPDC and DKBA troops, reporting that three of them fell down, believing that they had been killed. The first group which had been sent to attack the DKBA camp on the mountain found it empty; the soldiers had left it the night before to spend the night in Kyauk Kyi. But leaving their compound the night before didn't save them as they were the eight who haplessly walked right into Myint Oo's ambush.

The company regrouped that afternoon at a designated jungle camp and took a well-deserved rest. Thoo Lay, Zaw Naing and Pa Gaw Koh were further treated before heading back to headquarters and the nearest clinic, which was a three-day walk away. Despite their predicament, they remained in high spirits. Over the next three days, not only did they walk proud, but they walked with smiles on their faces, even laughing some of the time, as if making fun of their own misery. 'It doesn't matter,' one soldier said to me, trying to explain why they seemed oblivious to their painful reality. 'They were born to die.' I thought the explanation was quite harsh, but I didn't argue with him. I was too inspired to care. I made a promise to myself that the next time I was down and out, sad or pissed off at life, I would think back to this time and remember the smiling faces of those three wounded soldiers who had to walk for four days to get to the nearest clinic. Whatever my future problems might be, I doubted they would be any worse than that. It was time to put my life into perspective.

Headquarters was not the same as when we left it a month before. We returned to a village which was abandoned except for the lone figure of a man and his rifle. Guerrillas didn't come more hardcore than this man who had been guarding the village for over two weeks after the villagers had fled in fear of the impending Burmese offensive. The clinic was deserted too. Without a trace of disappointment, Thoo Lay and Zaw Naing took back their weapons (Pa Gaw Koh was already carrying his by this point), and disregarding their injuries, awaited their next operation. Clinics were a luxury they would have to do without. It was a harsh reminder of something Sheemoh had told me earlier. Before embarking on this trip, I had collected donations from five Japanese friends of mine to purchase medicine and take it into the Third Brigade area. The donation totaled 25,000 baht (about US$600 at the time), and Sheemoh and I went on a medical shopping spree in Mae Sot before embarking on our journey. While Sheemoh was thankful, he was quick to point out something he believed his people needed even more. 'Yes, we need medicine,' he said, 'but more importantly we need arms and ammunition; because without arms and ammunition, we will have no people to give medicine to.'

With the fall of their main trade gates in the late 1980s and early 90s, Manerplaw in January 1995, then their next biggest base of Wangkha the following month, the KNLA and KNU have seen their sources of income dwindle to the point of desperation. They receive no international support except for charitable donations by some individuals, private groups, or NGOs (particularly Christian groups), which are generally for humanitarian supplies such as medicine. Their main source of income comes from taxation in the areas they control, which is their primary source of income for buying arms and ammunition, purchased from their connections in the Thai military. The soldiers of the KNLA receive no salary; its force of around 5,000 fighters are all volunteers. Many of their weapons are more than 30 years old; I've even seen some soldiers go into battle with rifles from World War Two.

Some of their weapons are even homemade. Their own version of a Claymore mine is made by filling plastic boxes with steel balls, while landmines are fashioned from empty bottles of energy drinks filled with explosives and battery-powered detonators. 'Nobody is helping us,' Ner Dah once said to me, 'we're using homemade Claymores, we're using homemade landmines and we have some armories at work attempting to modify some old weapons. If we got 5,000 weapons tomorrow, we could free our people.' But the international community idly stands by, criticizing the junta and emposing sanctions, while the Karen defend their homeland and brave the onslaught of a 400,000-strong army with plastic Tupperware and empty bottles of Redbull. And they will keep on fighting for their freedom, according to Ner Dah, 'until one day the Burmese soldiers say, "you deserve it, we'll give it to you".'

Landmines are used extensively by the KNLA whose use of them reveals some sobering truths about this controversial weapon which is banned by more than 125 countries. Not only is it a very effective weapon for a guerrilla army, but it can also help protect lives. The KNLA uses landmines primarily for defensive purposes in order to guard not just their military camps but also Karen villages and the civilian population who live in fear of the Burmese military.

'We have to use [landmines] for self-defense, to protect ourselves because they [the Burmese] outnumber us,' Ner Dah once explained to me. 'If we don't use landmines, [Burmese soldiers] can easily walk into Karen villages and they will keep on burning [them] …To protect our villages, it is necessary to use landmines.'

The weapon not only provides a crucial line of defense by stalling Burmese advances, but it also serves as a type of alarm system to alert villagers and the KNLA of the presence of Burmese soldiers in an area. If an explosion is heard, a KNLA unit will be sent into the area to look for enemy activity. If enemy activity is discovered, then the villagers will have enough time to evacuate their village and flee to the jungle where they will hide until it is safe to return.

'Without landmines, we would not exist,' Sheemoh once told me.

Costing just a few dollars to make with ingredients that are readily available in any town, the landmine is a cash-starved guerrilla army's best friend: they're easy to make, easy to carry, and despite what critics of the weapon may argue, they are a very effective weapon of war, especially for armies who lack the manpower to defend and hold on to territory. In 52 BC, the Roman Army defeated a Gallic force more than five times its size by fortifying its positions with primitive landmines. More recently, landmines contributed to approximately 33 percent of all US casualties during the Vietnam War—a major factor behind the success of communist guerrillas in Indochina. As a Khmer Rouge general once said, a landmine is a perfect soldier, 'Ever courageous, it never sleeps and it never misses.' And while the Khmer Rouge was a contemptible force, they were a very successful guerrilla group.

The psychological impact of landmines on enemy forces also contributes towards their effectiveness. Causing horrific injuries that are intended to maim instead of kill their victims, the threat of stepping on a landmine is a constant source of dread for any soldier. As a volunteer mercenary in the KNLA once told me, 'I'm not afraid of being shot or killed, I'm just afraid of stepping on a mine.' The KNLA claims that the fear of stepping on landmines greatly discourages the Burmese army from patrolling beyond their base camps, and KNLA commanders have repeatedly told me that their heavy use of landmines is the main deterrent of Burmese attacks.

Of course, the landmine is a horrific weapon that shows its brutality in the countless numbers of Karen soldiers and civilians who are missing limbs because of it; but weapons are not made for their pleasantness.

And while the landmine does not discriminate between combatants and civilians, neither does the Burmese army. Furthermore, unlike professionally manufactured landmines that remain active for decades, and continue to kill and maim people long after conflicts have ended, the Karen's homemade mines have a soil life of about six months—the amount of time it takes for the batteries to die. In no way do I support the widespread use of landmines; neither do I deny the horrific consequences of the weapon, but to ban it is to disregard the plight of peoples such as the Karen who, having limited resources, depend on it for their survival. Besides, small arms like the AK-47 kill over 15 times more people a year than landmines kill and injure combined.

At the abandoned headquarters of the KNLA's ninth battalion in early March 2001, landmines were stalling the advance of the Burmese army's 11th and 905th battalions. By the time we arrived back there after almost a month, 2,257 Karen villagers were living as IDPs in the nearby jungle. The nearest camp from the headquarters of Ler Wah was just a few kilometers away, where the villagers were hiding. It was the first of several IDP camps I passed through that week as Tee Poh guided me back to the Thai border. I was leaving after seven weeks in Karen State, and all I could think about was crossing back into Thailand, having a beer and eating a pizza. But misery would meet me every part of the way before then, beginning within an hour of the five-day journey back to the 'land of smiles'.

Deep in the jungle near a small stream, the villagers of Ler Wah were living in hammocks and mats on the forest floor, waiting to either return to their village or to flee again, depending on the movements of the Burmese soldiers. When Tee Poh and I arrived, women were cooking over open fires, small children were gathering firewood, many were just resting and waiting, sitting in their hammocks or on the ground, all their belongings packed beside them in bamboo baskets ready to move at a moment's notice. 'Born to run,' Gee Gi once told me, describing his people with a tragic smile on his face. 'The Karen people are born to run—run for their lives.'

One woman in the camp, aged in her 40s, was lying sick on a mat on the ground with an intravenous tube in her forearm hooked up to a water bottle which was tied to a small bamboo tree above her. I don't know what she was suffering from or what treatment she was being given, but the effort to treat her was nothing less than remarkable. The Karen are no amateurs at survival.

After resting and using one of my last rolls of film, Tee Poh and I continued on to our day's destination, a small village about eight hours away. Yet another blister was beginning to form on the heel of my foot, which in a few days would swell almost to the size of a golf ball, providing me with one last souvenir of pain. But in terms of physical exhaustion, the journey out was much easier than the journey in, as by now I had lost close to ten kilos and was in pretty good shape. With Thailand and all its pleasures before me as a motivation, I blocked the pain of my swollen foot and trudged on, singing songs in my head and dreaming of crossing the Salween River and arriving in the Thai town of Mae Sariang. Then only Mae Sot remained before I would reach Bangkok.

In the late afternoon of the second day of the journey back to Thailand, we arrived at the KNU's district headquarters of Baw Kaw. We had passed through it over a month before, and it was nice to see some familiar faces, especially that of a man named Saw Htoo Paw, the district's finance secretary. He was a man in his 50s and was able to speak English; I took an immediate liking to him as he was quite a character. I would meet him several more times over the next two years, spending Christmas with him in 2002 and staying several nights with him and his family in their dilapidated house. Despite their bleak existence, he was always in good spirits and always made me laugh.

'Nelson, would you like some lunch?' he began on one occasion.

'No thanks, I've already eaten,' I replied.

'Good, because all I have are cucumbers.'

Another time we were talking about marijuana (although neither of us smoked it and the KNU is staunchly against drugs), but I didn't understand him at first because he was pronouncing it 'marajoona'. When I finally realized what he was saying, I corrected his mistake in pronunciation. He looked at me in disbelief before he smiled and replied, 'You mean I've been pronouncing it wrong for the last 30 years?' We both had a good laugh.

Saw Htoo Paw had spent much of his adult life in the jungle resisting the Burmese and dedicating his life to his people. But he was tired. I could tell he wanted nothing more than for the war to end. 'We don't want to fight any more,' he told me, 'we want to set up schools, hospitals, training schools, and have a free life.' But despite his desire for peace, giving up was not an option.

'Surrender is out of question,' he would say, citing one of the four principles outlined by the KNU's founding father, Saw Ba U Gyi, who was shot dead by Burmese troops in August 1950. (The other three principles are: we shall retain our arms, we shall decide our own political destiny and the recognition of Karen State must be completed.)

'If we don't continue to fight, we will be slaves,' Saw Htoo Paw explained. 'We do our best ... God helps those who help themselves.'

I admired his faith and unwarranted optimism, but, having lived among such a selfless people, I must admit that I never saw any evidence in Karen State to back up that saying.

Tee Poh and I spent the night at Saw Htoo Paw's headquarters, sleeping in hammocks on raised, open-air bamboo structures, with the stars forming the ceiling above us. Saw Htoo Paw, myself, and a few other English-speaking teachers and leaders talked well into the night, all of them thrilled to get a chance to speak English while I enjoyed my first conversation with more than one person who could speak English in over a month. But in the back of my mind, I was tired of hearing about their hardships and their miseries. I was getting accustomed to it—it was becoming the norm. By now, I didn't even think IDP camps were all that bad, because in their village they had little more. And the refugee camps in Thailand were like luxurious resorts compared to the villages and camps that were left behind. Hardship and misery is all a matter of perspective.

On the morning of the third day on the journey back to Thailand, we arrived at Gee Gi's command post where we stopped to eat and rest. By now, Tee Poh and I had been joined by about ten other soldiers and civilians who were also making the trek back to Thailand, including two teachers from Saw Htoo Paw's headquarters. They both spoke fluent English and it was great to have them as companions for the rest of the way, especially since Tee Poh and I were only able to communicate via sign language, a few words of Karen, and a lot of guessing.

It was nice to see Gee Gi again and he was happy to see me, but I had to refuse his invitation to spend the night as all I wanted to do was get back to Thailand as soon as possible. Staying the night would delay my exit by a day, and by now I was counting the hours until I left Karen State. After eating, he walked us to the Bellin River about twenty minutes away where we shook hands and said goodbye. I told him I'd be back again at the beginning of the dry season, but it would be nearly two years before I returned to his area and saw him again. When I did, I spent about two weeks at his home, passing the time talking, reading, sipping coffee, and listening to 60s music on his battery-powered tape recorder.

During that same trip, Gee Gi and I spent a night in the small village of Day Baw Key a few day's walk away as he accompanied me to a frontline area in Third Brigade with about 40 other soldiers from the ninth battalion. When we entered the village, a man and his pregnant wife, who was several days overdue, invited us to their home. The concerned couple asked me if I had any medicine to induce labor. Apologetically I said I did not, but assured them not to worry and that everything would probably be fine. A couple of hours later the wife went into labor and gave birth to a healthy baby boy. I guess they thought I brought them good luck, for they named their son 'Nelson Came'. We left the next day, but in a way I never really left.

When Gee Gi wasn't gathering intelligence on enemy troop movements, he spent his spare time studying subjects such as finance, management, and law. Even though he was in his 50s and lived on the run in the jungle, the veteran rebel was pursuing a diploma in International Issues through an Australian distance education program. Course books were sent from Australia to an address in Mae Sot, where someone would hand deliver them to a refugee camp, from which they'd be hand-carried into his area through rebel networks. I thought it was amazing how a guerrilla fighter in one of the most remote war zones in the world could pursue such an education. What was more amazing to me, however, was Gee Gi's desire to do so. His thirst for knowledge and education was inspiring, and seeing him at night studying under the dim, flickering flame of a small candle was a major motivator for me to further my own education and pursue a Master's degree two years later.

I acquired this picture of Pol Pot from an RCAF soldier who had found it in a deserted Anlong Veng house.

The picture immediately gripped me: here was one of history's most prolific killers portrayed in a completely different light: as a loving, caring man.

Pol Pot (middle) with Ieng Sary (left) and Son Sen (right) most likely in China in the early 1980s. I also acquired this picture, and the one below, in Anlong Veng in late April 1998.

Khieu Samphan (second from left) dining with Monineath Sihanouk, the wife of Norodom Sihanouk, most likely in Thailand in the 1980s.

The author at the KNLA's Walaykey base camp during an all night watch as KNLA guerrillas received intelligence of an imminent attack on the camp, December 2000.

Above: An alleged spy is chained by KNLA guerrillas at Walaykey base camp, December 2000.

Karen soldiers keep watch from a trench during the attack on Tojo, November 2000.

Karen guerrillas of the ninth battalion head back to base after ambushing a column of Burmese government soldiers, January 2003.

Karen Internally Displaced Persons, February 2002.

Betrayed and forgotten: Hmong guerillas in Xaysomboune Special Zone, April 2004. If there was an international index of persecuted peoples, then the Hmong would rank among the top.

Nhia Lo Vang, a Hmong guerrilla who lost his foot in a landmine blast in 1997, and 6-year-old Meng Lor at a camp in Xaysomboune Special Zone, April 2004.

Hmong guerrillas dig up tree roots, their staple diet, Xaysomboune Special Zone, April 2004.

Moua Thoua Ther using his satellite phone to inform Hmong-Americans of my successful arrival, Xaysomboune Special Zone, April 2004.

For the jungle Hmong on the run, the very old, as well as the very young, have no other choice but to bear arms to defend themselves.

Major Somkid Konkaeng (left) goes over a patrol route with one of his platoon commanders, Second-Lieutenant Kosin Soha, in Yaha district of Yala, southern Thailand, March 2008.

The CS Pattani Hotel the day after militants bombed it on 15 March 2008. Two people were killed and over a dozen were injured.

Gee Gi had passed eight courses and had 12 more to go to receive his diploma before the books stopped coming. To this day, he doesn't know why the program stopped sending him the books, and he remains without his diploma. But he still has the books and reviews them regularly, often under candlelight on the wooden floor of his forest hut, hoping that one day the 12 remaining books will come. He may not have a diploma, but he has much to teach the world about life.

After saying goodbye to Gee Gi at the Bellin River in early March 2001, Tee Poh and I, along with the two teachers and several others who had joined us along the way, continued on towards the Thai border, which was still two and a half days away. From the rocky shores of the Bellin River we pushed on through the forest, navigating steep mountain slopes, rocky trails, thick vegetation, and narrow jungle pathways until we reached the site of another IDP camp in a picturesque jungle setting where we stopped for the night, sleeping among the dispossessed villagers, the majority of whom were children.

The next day was one of the most painful of my life. A massive blister had formed on my heel and was by now causing excruciating pain at every step. The only consolation was the thought of Thailand. With each step of pain, I kept telling myself I was one step closer. Aware of my agony, Tee Poh suggested we stop and spend the night in a village about three hours away from our target destination. But I vehemently refused his idea, knowing that this would prolong our journey by a day. There was no way I was going to let that happen. I sucked up the pain, blocked it out as much as I could, and focused on three things: Thailand, Thailand and Thailand. I limped into the village of Day Bu Noh, nestled in the valley of the Bu Tho mountain range on the shores of the Yunzalin River, late that afternoon with one foot wearing a jungle boot and the other a sandal. I was exhausted, scruffy, battered, and in agony, but rarely have I felt any better—I was now a day away from Thailand and Day Bu Noh had beer.

That evening, using a needle dipped in boiling water, Tee Poh miraculously drained all the fluid from my blistered foot as we prepared for the final leg of our journey to the Thai border. With the help of warm beer imported from Thailand, all of the day's pain and anguish simply drowned away. The steep mountain slope that awaited us on the outskirts of the village did little to dampen my mood, for nothing could be worse than the ordeal of the past two months, and in the slight chance that it would be, at the end of the day my entire ordeal would be over. Karen State and its miseries would finally be behind me. I didn't have much time to dwell over many more thoughts, for after two beers I was out cold.

Day Bu Noh was still in darkness when I was awoken by Tee Poh who was signaling that it was time to set out. With flashlights in hand, we left the village for the forest and began the long, arduous ascent up the mountain, the same mountain that I had struggled to descend two months beforehand. Amazingly, Tee Poh's rudimentary treatment of my blistered foot had made it almost completely better, the pain having abated significantly since the previous day. In the coolness of the night, the climb up the mountain was barely even a challenge, and we arrived at its peak well before sunrise. I was amazed at our progress and figured we would be in the Thai town of Mae Sariang for dinner, a wonderful prospect after 57 nights in the jungle.

Slowly, the jungle canopy began to brighten as the rising sun lifted itself above the mountains, producing an array of colors and sounds as nature awoke to the dawn of a new day. In more ways than one, I was walking through the darkness into the light. Before long, we were descending the final eastern slope of the Bo Tho range, crisscrossing our way down to the river valley below, which marked the natural border between Burma and Thailand, and between the rebel state of Kowthoolei and the peaceful Thai province of Mae Hong Son—two very different worlds. Walking down that mountain towards the Salween River, I was overcome by feelings of joy and pride at my accomplishment. The river had now become much more than just a border crossing to me. It was a marker of life.

Arriving in the Karen village of Mae Nu Tah on the banks of the Salween River that afternoon was one of the happiest moments of my life, with my face almost hurting from the constant smile on my bearded face. The high was temporarily lost when I was told we had to wait until the morning for a boat to smuggle me back into Thailand, but several Singha beers soon changed that. I bought a case to share with Tee Poh and my other walking companions to celebrate the end of the journey, but I knew it was only the end of the journey for me, for this was their life. Their journey, like their war, was not ending soon.

A few weeks before, when we were camped in the forest near Kyauk Kyi, several of us were sitting in a circle on the ground, including the company commander, Saw Kay, a highly dedicated soldier in his mid 40s who was, uncommonly, still single. As we talked about their struggle and our personal lives, he told me that he planned to get married when the war was over. Everyone in the group fell silent, and then burst into laughter. I was laughing too, but I didn't know whether we were laughing at the prospect of him never marrying, or of the war never ending.

Seven years later, at the time of writing, there is still no end in sight for the Karen's war. An informal pact was made between the SPDC and the KNLA/KNU to halt fighting after rare peace negotiations in December 2003, and a 'gentleman's agreement' was made for an open-ended ceasefire after a second round of talks in January 2004. However, talks soon broke down and the ceasefire, which was never fully adhered to, collapsed. In November 2005, Burmese government forces launched their biggest offensive in Karen State since 1997, which displaced over 27,000 Karen civilians over the next year and prompted more than 3,000 to flee to Thailand where they joined the already vast community of some 150,000 Karen who live as refugees in seemingly permanent camps on the Thai-Burmese border.

More worryingly for the KNLA and the KNU are the internecine struggles that continue to plague their movement, with recent internal strife at a level not seen since the early 1990s when U Thuzana's Buddhist followers rose up and split to form the DKBA. This time it's not a split along religious lines, but between those who favor to talk and make peace with the SPDC and those who prefer to fight. These divisions only serve to help Burma's ruling generals, who have long used a 'divide and conquer' strategy to weaken pro-democracy and armed resistance groups in the country.

In January 2007, the KNLA's Seventh Brigade commander, Major-General Htay Maung, struck a peace deal with the SPDC without the approval of the KNU's central committee and broke away with about 300 of his soldiers to form the KNU/KNLA Peace Council. The bold move came just after General Bo Mya, the Karen's long-time strongman and leader, died of illness on Christmas Eve 2006. The following August, the commander of the KNLA's 18th battalion, Lieutenant-Colonel Kyi Linn, was shot dead while crossing a river by boat in Karen State after secretly meeting with government and DKBA officials. The previous month, a friend of mine who worked as an intelligence officer in the KNLA, Major Tashee, was shot and killed outside a refugee camp in Thailand. In January 2008, Htay Maung's son-in-law, Colonel Ler Moo, was killed by a bomb placed under his bed near the headquarters of the KNU/KNLA Peace Council inside Karen State. While at the time of writing there has been no confirmation of who was responsible for these killings, speculation was rife that they were the result of Karen infighting. The KNU/KNLA Peace Council accused the KNU and its general-secretary, Padoh Mahn Sha, of masterminding Ler Moo's assassination.

A life-long resistance fighter, Mahn Sha was elected general-secretary of the KNU, the third highest position in the political group, at the KNU's 12th Congress in 2000. He quickly became the public face of the KNU and was well-respected among all of Burma's opposition groups, as throughout his career he worked hard to unify the myriad ethnic and political groups of the country's opposition forces. I interviewed him with Daniel Pedersen (an Australian journalist) in July 2001 after the two of us visited the scene of a DKBA attack on a Karen IDP camp just across the Thai border. When we asked Mahn Sha about the situation in Karen State that summer and the government's stepped-up military campaigns against the KNLA, he replied bluntly, 'They [Burmese troops] have been ordered to destroy everything, even the plants, so there is nothing left to sustain human life.'

Two weeks after Ler Moo's assassination, which the KNU/KNLA Peace Council accused Mahn Sha of ordering, I met with my old friend Tennyson at a popular Western restaurant in Mae Sot. In recent years, he has favored non-violent methods over continued warfare against the SPDC, and has travelled the world to raise awareness of the plight of the Karen. He even participated in the peace talks in Burma that led to the short-lived gentleman's ceasefire agreement in January 2004.

'By fighting, we get nothing,' he told me. 'Only lose, lose, lose.' He shared with me his long-thought-out alternative schemes for trying to defeat the SPDC, one of which was to flood the country with counterfeit money. No stranger to being on someone's hit list because of his swashbuckling ways, the recent infighting and assassination plots gave him even more reason to fear for his life, although he candidly told me that if he was killed he would like a medal to be awarded to his assassin. Nevertheless, he kept a machete beside him in his pick-up truck. 'I am a peace man,' he told me that night, 'but everyone wants to kill me.'

The next day, on 14 February 2008, two Karen men walked into Mahn Sha's house in Mae Sot, went upstairs where the 64-year-old general-secretary was resting on his balcony, greeted him, and then shot him dead. It was yet another loss in the Karen's endless struggle.

CHAPTER 3

LAOS AND VIETNAM:

THE PLIGHT OF AMERICA'S FORGOTTEN ALLIES

LAOS AND VIETNAM

I was nervous. The last journalists who had visited the area into which I was heading had been arrested and sentenced to 15 years in prison. The fact that they were released after 35 days in custody did little to calm my nerves as I arrived in Laos with over thirteen hundred dollars in cash, two cameras, military apparel, survival equipment and a solar panel battery charger—not the typical belongings of the tourist I was pretending to be. But I was willing to take the risk; after all, you never regret the things you do in life, only the things you *don't* do. Besides, after a year of planning and liaising with contacts in Thailand and America, plus almost ten years of studying the situation and dreaming about it, I wasn't going to back out of the opportunity to visit one of the world's least known armies.

I arrived in the northeastern Lao town of Phonsavan on 9 April 2004 with a set of simple instructions: go to the central market on the 11th and look for a man in black clothes, wearing a hat bearing the number 32. I was to refer to him only by that number, and he would be my guide who would lead me to ethnic Hmong guerrillas operating in the nearby hills. These were the remnants of a former CIA-backed army that had never surrendered after the communist takeover of Laos in 1975.

The instructions were given to me in Thailand by a man who I knew as TJ, a Hmong-American who fought for that same CIA army in the 1960s and 70s but eventually escaped to Thailand and later resettled in America. His heart never really left his war-torn homeland though, and he could not forget the thousands of other Hmong who never made it out. In 2001, he helped establish a network of Hmong agents in Laos called 'blackbirds' who could make contact with the guerrillas and smuggle items such as satellite phones and video cameras to them. This gave them a valuable means of communicating with the outside world while also enabling them to document their valiant struggle. Now TJ was using the blackbird network to smuggle journalists into these guerrilla groups, and I was next. My blackbird was Number 32.

I awoke early on 11 April, checked out of my guesthouse, and made my way to the central market to make contact with Number 32. Unfortunately, Phonsavan has two markets, both in the center of town, creating confusion for someone with instructions to meet a man known only by a number in the town's central market. I spent the next eight hours combing both marketplaces for any sign of the mysterious Number 32, carefully eyeing anyone in black with a hat. Frustrated and disappointed, I almost gave up my search until I finally spotted him late in the afternoon.

I expected a veteran operative who was experienced in clandestine activities, so I was completely surprised when Number 32 turned out to be a 12-year-old boy.

Like a scene out of a comical spy movie, the boy and his friends led me out of the market and into a back alley, pretending to be secret about it but doing obvious things like constantly looking back at me to make sure I was following them. Confused and astonished, I followed their lead wondering how in the world these kids were going to bring me to meet some of the toughest guerrillas on earth. But I kept my hopes up.

Once in the alley, we attempted to communicate in sign language and Thai, a similar language to Lao. I asked them if they were Hmong and they said yes. I then pretended to hold an automatic rifle and started shooting it, making sounds of gunfire and pointing to them, then to myself, and the mountains in the distance. I was trying to say, 'Can you take me to the Hmong guerrillas?'

Number 32 pointed to his neck and slid his finger across it, giving the universal sign for death. I took that as a no. Nevertheless, he wanted me to show him where I was staying in Phonsavan. So I led the boys to the guesthouse where I had stayed the previous two nights. When we were close enough to see it, I pointed to it and walked away, not wanting to draw attention to any potential onlookers or followers. I checked back in the guesthouse for another night, utterly disappointed at the day's events. There was only one thing to do: drown my disappointment with Beer Lao. So I headed into town and proceeded accordingly.

Phonsavan is a sleepy little town situated on the Xieng Khouang plateau in northeastern Laos. Thousands of mysterious stone jars litter the rolling hills of the surrounding countryside, relics of an unknown race that inhabited the area over two thousands years ago. During the Vietnam War, the town and surrounding plains became one of the most heavily bombed and contested areas in the history of warfare when American-backed forces battled the communist Pathet Lao and North Vietnamese Army. Having been utterly destroyed in the fighting, the town of Xieng Khouang was rebuilt in the mid 1970s and renamed Phonsavan. Today, an increasing number of tourists are finding their way to the town to get a glimpse of the jars and of the war paraphernalia that litter the countryside. Unbeknownst to most of them, only a short distance away in mountainous areas that are off-limits to foreigners, groups of mainly ethnic Hmong tribesmen and their family members are still fighting the last battles of that war.

I was probably on my second beer when a man approached me from the street with two boys in tow. They were the same boys from that afternoon, only this time the 12-year-old was not wearing a hat. The man sat down at my table, took off his cap, pointed to the number 32 on it, and handed me a note in English, 'Meet me here tomorrow at 6:30am, have your bags ready.' The real Number 32 had showed up, who I later found out was the older brother of the 12-year-old. Everything was now in place.

Number 32 appeared the next morning according to plan. This time, he gave me another note which said we would leave just before dark at 6pm. True to his word, he showed up at the designated restaurant exactly on time in an old beat-up car that had probably been around since the war. He handed me another note asking for petrol money and telling me to lie down in the back seat of the car during the journey so nobody would see me. I gave him $20, finished my dinner and off we went, driving into the darkness. I didn't know it at the time, but it would be almost a month until I returned to Phonsavan and the civilized world. It was a grueling journey that would change me forever.

I'm sure I could have caught a glimpse of a fading sunset over the distant hills as we left Phonsavan, but the only scenery available to me was the grungy floor of a beat-up car, reeking with petrol fumes. For 45 nerve-wracking minutes we traveled along dirt roads to reach a pre-arranged drop off site in the forbidden military zone of Xaysomboune. From here onwards, I could have faced a very long prison sentence for associating with the rebels, so it was imperative that I wasn't caught. This is what I was thinking when the car stalled shortly before our drop off site, pushing my heart rate into overdrive. Number 32 repeatedly tried to start the engine but to no avail. I'm not a religious man, but I found myself praying to God as seconds turned into an eternity in the back of that devilish car. It would not be my last cry for help over the next few weeks, and I even turned to Hmong sprits to help me through the ordeal. In times of danger, I can turn to any higher being.

I don't know if it was by God's help or the mechanical abilities of Number 32, but whatever it was seemed to work. Number 32 finally got the car started. The churning of the engine was music to my ears, and a relief to my pounding heart which had almost burst through my chest. Thankfully, we were on our way again.

A short while later, Number 32 handed me yet another note, 'When I count to three, you jump out of the car. One ... two ... three, you jump.' While he couldn't speak a word of English, his notes were quite well-written. I never found out who wrote them for him, but I figure it was one of the boys from the first day at the market who probably used a dictionary to translate the phrases word for word. Whoever it was did a pretty good job, but I wasn't thinking of praise for the quality of the English. I had much more pressing things to think about, like what would happen after I jumped out of the moving car and into the desolate night in the middle of a forbidden military zone.

Before I had much time to contemplate the madness of the situation, Number 32 started his count. 'One ... two ...,' but before he got to three he frantically motioned for me to stop. A car passed by in the opposite direction, a rarity in this area. This raised suspicion that it was a military vehicle, which forced us to abort the jump. But it passed by without stopping and, once the car was out of sight, Number 32 started his count again, 'One ... two ... three!' I opened the door of the moving car and jumped out just as another man emerged from the bushes to whisk me off the road. Number 32 drove off into the night, while the second man grabbed me by the arm and led me through an open rice field. I followed him at a frantic pace as he led me across the open field into a nearby forest. Once safely in the trees and out of sight of any roadside army patrol, my guide turned on his flashlight and slowed down into a more comfortable walk. I followed his lead and turned on my flashlight as well, relieved that we were out of immediate danger but still eerily aware of the risks that lurked at every footstep. It was an exhilarating rush.

Covered in mud and sweat, and consumed by fear and anticipation, I walked through the forest as my guide led me to the guerrillas. Somewhere in the distance, hiding in the forest's cover, they were waiting for my arrival. I didn't know how many there would be, or what to expect when I saw them, but I reveled in the realization that I was walking into history; straight into a war that was suppose to have ended in 1975—the year I was born.

After less than an hour of walking, my guide started to whistle. I knew from my experiences with other rebels in Southeast Asia that he was attempting to communicate with his comrades. Effective guerrillas need to be masters of their environment, to blend in and use their surroundings to their advantage. My guide was whistling in a way that only his comrades knew, and that any nearby enemy soldier would not be able to distinguish from the sound of a bird. It worked. Not long after my guide started his call sign, we got a response. It was another whistle, and we followed its sound.

Suddenly, the bushes started to rustle. Out of the darkness, eight armed men appeared on the jungle trail. One of the ghost-like figures was missing a hand,

and I immediately recognized him as the legendary commander Moua Thoua Ther, whose lower arm was shot off in battle in 1972. His uniform was battered and torn, and his face gave signs that his heart, though stalwart, had suffered similar mistreatment. The others faired no better, except that their limbs were all intact.

I hugged Moua Thoua Ther and his ragged men as one would greet long lost friends; not because I knew them, but because I knew their story. Here were eight men trapped in history, still fighting a war that officially ended three decades before. They had come to meet me and take me to their headquarters deep in the jungles of Xaysomboune, to show me their desperate community and the brutal war being waged against them. Since 1975, they had been holding out against the communist government of Laos, unable to flee and unwilling to surrender for fear of retribution and death. They were still fighting the last battles of the Vietnam War, and I was going to witness and document this tragic legacy, a secret to most of the world. I remember looking up into the night sky and rejoicing at my personal victory in reaching this God-forsaken group of guerrillas. Ever since I was a boy, the Vietnam War had fascinated me. I watched it in the movies, read about it, studied it, and wrote about it. Now, I was living it. For Moua Thoua Ther and his seven battered comrades, and for the Hmong hidden in the surrounding jungle, the Vietnam War had yet to end.

If there was an international index of persecuted peoples, then the Hmong would rank among the top. Originating in China with a culture that dates back over 4,000 years, centuries of war and persecution forced the Hmong to flee to remote mountainous areas where they adapted to the rigors of the Montagnard way of life. Resisting continuous attempts by the Chinese to take their lands and subjugate them, the Hmong engaged in several uprisings which led to several brutal campaigns against them. Determined to suppress them, the Chinese forbade the Hmong to use their written script—a crime made punishable by death. They also split them into groups and forced them to wear identifying clothing as a way of branding them. One Manchu emperor in the 18th century was so infuriated at the Hmong's resistance to his rule that he vowed to exterminate them. The communist government of Laos would make a similar vow two centuries later. The Hmong are probably the only race in the world that have been the target of two extermination attempts by two different states.

In order to escape the 18th century Chinese on-slaught, thousands of Hmong fled southward to present-day Vietnam, Laos, Burma and Thailand. Fiercely independent, they remained out of the control of central governments, preferring to live in isolated communities high in the rugged mountains of their new homelands.

When the French arrived in Indochina in the late 1800s and established colonial rule over Vietnam, Cambodia and Laos, the Hmong were one of the first to revolt. Led by a messianic figure named Pa Chay who was believed to have possessed magical abilities, rebels under his command attacked French forces with crossbows, flintlocks, homemade artillery and rocks in a four-year insurrection that extended across both Vietnam and Laos. While the French eventually defeated the rebels in 1921, it was a remarkable example of guerrilla warfare that would later define the tactics of war in Indochina. The French must have been impressed for the next time war broke out in the region they immediately recruited the Hmong.

During the latter stages of Word War Two, when France and the Allied Forces began operations to take back Indochina from the Japanese, French commandos recruited Hmong from the highlands of Laos to serve as guides, messengers, interpreters, porters and guerrilla fighters. Armed with the latest weapons and technology, the Hmong stepped out of the stone age and into the harsher age of global warfare and superpower politics. They had the misfortune of inhabiting one of the most strategically important areas of 20th century warfare, and they are still facing the consequences to this day.

Having demonstrated their prowess in battle during the successful campaign against the Japanese, the Hmong played an integral role in France's eight-year war against Vietnam's communist Viet Minh from 1946 to 1954. They formed the backbone of a guerrilla army to resist invading Viet Minh forces as the Vietnamese communists sought to take over parts of northern Laos to extend their strategic influence and control, as well as to seek sanctuary from French forces in northern Vietnam. The Hmong became masters at hit-and-run tactics and their intimate knowledge of the land made them extremely effective guerrilla fighters. When 14,000 French forces were pinned down and surrounded by 50,000 Viet Minh troops in the Vietnamese town of Dien Bien Phu in 1954, it was the Hmong who tried to rescue them. Two thousand guerrillas trekked for over 20 days to try and help their besieged comrades, but Dien Bien Phu fell before the team could arrive. The guerrillas helped dozens of French soldiers escape from the area and even stayed on to search for survivors, saving at least 200 of them from certain death. About 2,000 Hmong were taken prisoner in the battle for Dien Bien Phu or captured in the surrounding hills, including a young man named Yang Mi Cha. He would become one of the longest held prisoners of war in history, spending the next 25 years in prison in Vietnam. No one ever tried to secure his release.

The French defeat at Dien Bien Phu marked the end of France's colonial adventures in Indochina. But it also marked the beginning of a new era of confrontation. The United States and its allies were eager to contain the spread of communism in the region so, as French forces moved out, the Americans started to move in. The Hmong would once again be pulled into the conflict both because of their strategic location in which they lived and for their capabilities as skilled mountain guerrillas. Like the French, the Americans used the Hmong to resist the invading Vietnamese communist forces, as well as a growing communist insurgency in Laos being conducted by the Vietnamese-backed Pathet Lao.

By the late 1950s, Laos had become one of the hottest frontlines in the Cold War. US military personnel had begun operating covertly in Laos in 1957, training and leading indigenous forces to attack communist positions. The Soviet Union and China backed the Lao communists and the North Vietnamese, who began infiltrating Laos in order to build a network of trails for sending troops and supplies to aid their insurgency in South Vietnam. Collectively known as the Ho Chi Minh Trail, nearly all of the 12,500 miles of track was on Laotian soil. In the country's northeast, the armed wing of the Lao communists, the Pathet Lao, were gaining ground and had firm control over the two provinces of Phong Saly and Sam Neua.

In order to halt this communist expansion in Laos, the United States secretly recruited a guerrilla force consisting primarily of Hmong tribesmen from the mountainous province of Xieng Khouang. Funded by the CIA in order to conceal America's involvement, this clandestine guerrilla force grew from a paramilitary organization consisting of a few hundred soldiers to an army of nearly 40,000 soldiers with its own air force. The leader of this secret army was a charismatic Hmong general named Vang Pao, who as a teenager served as a translator and messenger for French commandos. In 1954, he was one of the 2,000 guerrillas that attempted to rescue the doomed French soldiers trapped at Dien Bien Phu. When I returned after visiting his abandoned army in the mountains of Xaysomboune in 2004, he held a ceremony for me in Sacramento, California to congratulate me on my feat. He even slaughtered a goat on my behalf to honor the Hmong spirits that kept me safe. He knew that I had narrowly missed a Laotian army outpost as I was being escorted out of the jungle by Moua Thoua Ther's men. 'If I was a Lao soldier at that outpost,' he told me at the ceremony, 'you'd be dead.'

Indeed, General Vang Pao was a brilliant guerrilla fighter and leader who helped to hold back an ever-expanding force of North Vietnamese and Pathet Lao insurgents for over ten years. He was constantly in the field commanding his troops, occasionally even leading them into battle. While he had a ruthless side, he was mostly well-loved and respected among his people and is regarded by many as a hero. Soft-spoken and charming, he had the canny ability to influence and lead. When I met him in California, I was drawn to him because of these traits and took an immediate liking to him. I asked him about Dien Bien Phu and told him that I used to live in Vietnam. I even mentioned that I had a Vietnamese girlfriend when I lived there, and he replied with a smile, 'Oh yes, I had one of those too.' He may have been a hardcore guerrilla fighter, but he had a soft side as well.

By 1962, the majority of US assistance to anti-communist forces in Laos was going directly to Vang Pao and his guerrillas. Over the next ten years, about $20 billion was spent on Vang Pao's army, the single largest enterprise of the CIA ever. The guerrillas gathered intelligence, rescued downed American pilots, and defended navigational sites which enabled the US to carry out all-weather bombing raids against North Vietnam and communist forces in northern Laos. They also regularly engaged the Pathet Lao and North Vietnamese in battle. While the Hmong constituted the majority of the guerrilla force, ethnic Lao and other highland minorities such as the Khmu and Yao were also among the ranks.

Although Vang Pao's army was a formidable force that had mastered the art of guerrilla warfare, it had one major disadvantage compared with the communists: a serious lack of manpower. Even at the height of the war, when about 80 percent of all Hmong of fighting age were the soldiers of Vang Pao, their numbers paled in comparison to the North Vietnamese, who were prepared to suffer enormous casualties for their cause. In the end, it was a war the Hmong could not win. Unable to hold captured territory and defend against waves of assaults, the best they could hope for was to survive. But many didn't. The Hmong paid dearly for their efforts in a war that wasn't even their own. For helping the Americans, about 17,000 Hmong fell in battle, and another 50,000 non-combatants died from crossfire, disease, and starvation as entire villages were forced to flee into remote highland areas to avoid advancing communist forces. Nearly all Hmong in Xieng Khouang became refugees at one point or another during the war, and no one was left unscathed by the conflict.

In the 1970s, American support slowly began to dwindle until it eventually ceased altogether, leaving the Hmong to fend for themselves. It was an impossible task. In May 1975, facing imminent defeat by the communists, Vang Pao disbanded his army and fled to Thailand with 5,000 of his followers. Just days before his departure, a Pathet Lao newspaper vowed to exterminate the Hmong people 'down to the root'. This was no empty threat; the communists were completely serious. Over three decades later and the government of Laos is still heeding this promise.

When Vang Pao fled to Thailand in May 1975, Moua Thoua Ther, the man who would meet me in the jungle in April 2004, was just 17 years old. He had already been a soldier in the CIA's secret army for five years. During a fierce battle in 1972, when he was only 14 years old, his left hand was shot off by enemy fire. Recalling the battle to me 32 years later, he said that all the Hmong in the village had to take up arms to fight off that attack, even the young girls. He said they would have lost the battle if it wasn't for a US bombing raid that annihilated the attackers just in time. Although maimed in the battle, Moua Thoua Ther escaped death, something he'd excel at over the next three decades.

Thousands of Hmong were later herded into concentration camps following the communist takeover of Laos in 1975. As thousands more fled to neighboring Thailand to escape persecution, Moua Thoua Ther fled deep into the mountainous jungles of Xieng khouang accompanied by over a thousand others. Having chosen to fight on, they dug up weapons and ammunition they had earlier buried.

'We thought the Americans would surely come back and help us,' he told me three decades later while still on the run in the jungle. 'But they never did.'

Moua Thoua Ther's group was just one of many that took to the hills in 1975 to organize the resistance against the new regime. With family members in tow, these groups probably amounted to around 75,000 people, about 15,000 of whom were armed men and boys. Most of them were concentrated around Phu Bia mountain in southeastern Xieng Khouang province, the highest mountain range in the area. Some of these warriors were there by choice, as they believed they could eventually defeat the communists; but most, like Moua Thoua Ther, were there because they had no other alternative. Unable to flee to Thailand like thousands of others because the communists had 'blocked the way', and not wanting to risk life in the concentration camps, Moua Thoua Ther and many like him chose the jungle.

Life in the jungle was difficult. Without the support of the United States, they no longer had the backing of air strikes, the luxury of being airlifted into other areas, or the opportunity to return to base camps to get supplies. They were completely on their own, facing an enemy that had the manpower, weapons and desire to slaughter every last man, woman and child. In these desperate times, many of them turned to a mystical group that promised not only to protect them from enemy forces, but also to give them the powers to destroy them. These mystical Hmong warriors called themselves *Chao-Fa* ('Prince of the Sky'). Their initial success on the battlefield after the communist takeover of Laos transformed many Hmong into die-hard followers of the group. Moua Thoua Ther, however, was not a convert. He chose instead to rely on the powers of his instinct and of his American-issued rifle.

By 1977, *Chao Fa* and other Hmong resistance groups had achieved several battlefield victories and were occupying a number of old CIA airstrips in the mountains of Xieng Khouang. The Lao and Vietnamese retaliated by launching a massive military offensive which included the use of chemical poisons. The US State Department identified the poisons as trichothecene mycotoxins and nerve gases; the Hmong who had escaped to Thailand simply called it 'yellow rain,' describing its appearance as it fell from the sky from enemy warplanes.

By 1980, the Hmong had begun to lose all hope of defeating the communists. The now toxic forests of Phu Bia could no longer be used as a sanctuary by the rebel army. Furthermore, the magical warriors of *Chao-Fa* were all but crushed, and the resistance was stripped of any hope that a supernatural agent would come to their salvation. From now on, they would have to count on ordinary men like Moua Thoua Ther.

By now, about 100,000 Hmong had fled Laos for Thailand. While no official casualty list existed, tens of thousands had perished in the five turbulent years from 1975 to 1980. Many of these had died while trying to make the grueling trek to Thailand. Another 2,000 Hmong still remained in detention for their wartime services to America and to Vang Pao. Among these was a man named Ly Dang. He was held at a detention center at Nong Het near the Vietnamese border where he endured indoctrination sessions, beatings and forced labor. He was held there for eight years before being released in 1983, no longer considered a threat to the state. His jailors were wrong. Three years later in 1986, in fear that he would be sent back to prison, Dang fled to the jungle where he eventually hooked up with Moua Thoua Ther. Using his military experience gained from six years in the CIA's secret army, Dang took up arms again and became a valuable member of Moua Thoua Ther's jungle force. Eighteen years later in 2004, the 50-year-old veteran guerrilla would help guide me to and from their jungle dwellings in the mountains of Xaysomboune. He had that hardcore look about him, just like Moua Thoua Ther, the kind of look that exudes a relentless will to survive. These are the kind of men you want beside you when you go into battle.

Throughout the 1980s, the Hmong resistance was able to stay alive due to limited outside support from Thailand and a trickle of covert support from the United States. Vang Pao was also able to raise funds by appealing to the Hmong community in the United States, which by the late 1980s totalled over 100,000 people. While no longer a serious threat to the government of Laos, Hmong resistance groups, like that of Moua Thoua Ther, could still launch attacks, capture territory, and control enough land to grow crops and raise animals. But when the Cold War ended and governments like that of Thailand chose to turn the battlefields of Indochina into marketplaces, the limited outside support dried up and left the Hmong once again on the wrong side of history. Since then, the Hmong resistance has become nothing more than a battle for survival.

It was this battle for survival that I wanted to witness and document in April 2004. This was a little over a year after two journalists, Philip Blenkinsop and Andrew Perrin, had first broken the story, bringing the miseries of Moua Thoua Ther's Hmong to the pages of *Time* magazine. Two months after their gripping article was published, two other foreign journalists reached Moua Thoua Ther's group but were caught on their way out. Thierry Falise and Vincent Reynaud were arrested along with their Hmong-American translator and three Hmong guides—one of whom was Moua Thoua Ther's son. They were sentenced to 15 years in prison on trumped up charges in connection with the killing of a security official. Falise, Reynauld and the translator were released after 35 days in custody but the Hmong guides were not so fortunate. Two of them will most likely serve their entire sentences; the other never even heard his verdict as he escaped from the toilet of a police guardhouse two days after his arrest. Va Char Yang fled back to Moua Thoua Ther's jungle hideout and was one of the eight men that met me in the forest ten months later. This time, he was packing a pistol.

It was a clear, beautiful night in the Laotian jungle as the eight guerrillas and I set out into the mountains under the cover of darkness. We needed to cover as much ground as possible before daylight in order to distance ourselves from any nearby government soldiers. The location where Moua Thoua Ther and his men met me at the jungle's edge was especially dangerous territory for them, although anywhere in their jungle abode was considered risky. Between them, they had three AK-47 assault rifles, an American-made M-16, an American-made M-79 grenade launcher, two rifles and a pistol.

They had only enough ammunition to fire a few shots and then run if attacked by the enemy. To make matters even worse, their weapons and ammunition were over 30 years old and frequently misfired, jammed, or simply did nothing. The only real advantages they had over their enemy were their intimate knowledge of the terrain and their will to survive. Not liking the odds, I was pinning my chances on the hope that Laotian soldiers liked to sleep.

We trekked through the darkness, negotiating thick jungle and hilly terrain that would have been difficult in daylight, let alone at night. I was no stranger to grueling jungle treks with rebels, so I put my mind into jungle mode. I blocked out the pain, blocked out the exhaustion and escaped the situation through the channels of my mind. But I was still very wary of every step and every corner taken. It's a delicate balancing act between awareness and escapism.

It was almost dawn and we had been walking for about five hours when we came across a small jungle clearing. It was here the guerrillas stopped and set up a small camp, building lean-to shelters out of bamboo and palm leaves. In a matter of minutes, enough shelters were erected for the eight of us to crawl inside and enjoy a brief sleep before daylight. We weren't asleep for long when we were awoken by a light rain shower, reminding me that it was the beginning of the rainy season. Jungle living is hard enough in the dry season, but when it rains it becomes miserable. Trails wash up and turn into mud flows, while personal comfort is replaced by what seems to be a constant wetness. Guerrillas, on the other hand, generally welcome the rains for they usually result in a let-up of government attacks due to the harsher conditions and the greater difficulty of manoeuvring through the mud-soaked jungles. For a journalist carrying a camera and video equipment though, the rains are not as welcome.

My first morning in the jungle with the Hmong was an eye-opening experience. One of the first things I saw was Va Char Yang, the Hmong guide who escaped from captivity ten months before, eating raw bird's eggs right out of their nest. Another man was sewing his pants together with bits of jungle vine. Other guerrillas had begun digging massive holes, which I initially thought were for bunkers in case we got attacked. It wasn't until they began to pull tree roots from the holes that I realized they were searching for food. Breakfast that morning was their staple meal, the food that has kept them alive for most of the 21st century: boiled tree roots. Before we ate, Moua Thoua Ther made an offering of roots to the spirits in the forest to keep us safe. I was just hoping the spirits wouldn't get angry at the meager food he was offering them.

After eating, the guerrillas disassembled the camp as quickly as they had set it up, removing any evidence that could give away our existence. We then continued on through the mountains to reach their jungle headquarters, which was still a few days walk away. We only trekked for about two hours that day, climbing a steep mountain before descending down to a river in the valley where we set up another camp for the night. It was here I first got to know one of the guerrillas, See Xeng Ly, a 46-year-old ex-CIA soldier who fled to the jungle in 1975. Since then, the nearest he had come to being out of the jungle was the previous night when he met me at the jungle's edge. He was but an hour's walk away from another world and another life.

Ly had learned some English before 1975, and now, for the first time in 29 years, he was able to put it to use. He told me his brother died in battle in 1990, and showed me a logbook of every battle he had been involved in since 1975. 'Fifty-seven battles,' he told me, and had the dates of each one in his notebook to prove it. When I later noticed that his battle numbers and dates weren't corresponding, I realized he was confusing the word 'battle' with 'attack'. 'Fifty-seven' was only the number of times he had attacked the enemy, while he was on the defensive side another 65 times. His battle total was actually 122.

We set out early the next morning, crossing the fast-moving, waist-deep river before navigating through another mountain pass. After a difficult climb to the 4,500-foot-high summit, we reached an old CIA landing strip which was littered with bullet and mortar rounds from a fierce battle for the hill in 1972. During the war, hundreds of such airstrips were constructed, usually on hilltops or mountain ridges, so the CIA could fly in supplies for Vang Pao's army, disperse aid, and transport troops and refugees. These crude landing strips were called 'Lima Sites', and each one was given a number. This particular strip was Lima Site 238 which was overrun by communist forces in 1972. When we arrived at the abandoned airstrip, the guerrillas combed through the war relics to see if there was anything of use. Va Char Yang found an

American-issued combat shovel for which he rejoiced, and most of the others grabbed a rusty, metal shell casing which could function as a container. When you have nothing, anything is useful.

The afternoon sun scorched down on us as we left Lima Site 238, with the guerrillas having taking anything that might be of use. No American planes were landing on the strip anymore, and there was no longer any prospect of outside support arriving. I envied the guerrillas I was with not for their situation, but for their fortitude to fight on in spite of it. I may have been following the most pathetic guerrilla force in the world, but I was walking amongst extraordinary men who could turn scraps of metal into prized possessions.

Despite already being loaded down with several kilos of equipment that was strapped to their backs in torn bags held together with jungle vine, the guerrillas added their newfound items and continued on, undeterred by the added weight. We descended the mountainside and melted back into the jungle's canopy, pushing on to reach the guerrilla headquarters which was still several kilometers away.

Later that day we were met by more of Moua Thoua Ther's men. They were dispatched from headquarters to escort us on the final leg of our journey. Ly Dang, who escaped to the jungle in 1986 after spending eight years in prison, was part of this escort team. He had a look that personified survival, but I'm sure he's more familiar with death. I took an immediate liking to him.

Dang was recruited into the CIA's secret army in 1969 when he was just 15 years old. At the age of 21, he was one of about 40,000 Laotians who were sent to 'seminar camps' after the communist takeover of Laos. At these seminar camps, officers, soldiers, police, and high officials of the previous regime were indoctrinated on communist ideology and on the revolution that they had tried to thwart. As one can imagine, they weren't pleasant places, and the term 'seminar' was just a polite substitute for prison. Inmates received little food, were used for forced labor and lived in harrowing conditions, often in mountain caves. Conditions in the jungle couldn't have been much better for Dang than they had been when he was in prison; but at least in the jungle he was free. This, however, didn't prevent his cries of desperation.

'Help us get out of here so we don't starve to death,' he pleaded with me. 'We don't want to die.'

We set up camp for the night in a small clearing which was swarmed with bees. As usual, the guerrillas wandered off into the forest to hack down bamboo trees with their machetes and to fetch giant palm leaves to build temporary shelters for the night. Others went searching for food, and came back with a giant beehive. Like joyful children, the guerrillas scooped up the thick honey with their hands and ate the hardened bristle of the hive with gleaming smiles, savoring the sweetness of their jungle treat. It was a pleasant change from the bitter roots.

We packed up early the next morning and set off for the final day of the trek to reach their jungle headquarters. Before we got far, the guerrillas stopped to try and fetch one more beehive before leaving the bee-infested area. One of the guerrillas climbed half way up a tree, carved out a small hole with his machete, and then poked away with his knife to try and find the illusive beehive. In order to strengthen his grip, the other guerrillas fashioned a ladder out of three bamboo sticks and some jungle vine. They then propped it against the tree so he could stand firm as he hacked away in search of the hive. Despite his valiant effort, the poor guerrilla came up with nothing; so we proceeded on into the jungle abyss, honey-less.

After about five hours, we arrived at a small mountain river that meandered its way through the jungle valley which stretched out before us. I knew we were close. For the first time in three days, I saw Hmong women and other signs of civilian life, although I wouldn't call their lives civil. They were searching for food, digging up roots and collecting anything they could eat. The Hmong have always been a subsistent people, but now they have been reduced to eating the food that even animals would avoid. I was approaching a community of nearly 2,000 people who were living off trees to survive. About two weeks later, Moua Thoua Ther broke down in the jungle and burst into tears as he was telling me of their dire situation. Here was one of the most hardened guerrillas on the planet, missing his left hand, and living on the run in the jungle for 29 years, crying like a baby, trying to comprehend why nobody in the world would help his people, not even the United Nations, an institution he regards as almost godlike—he's heard so much about it and its purported powers, but he's never actually seen it or seen what it has done.

'The United Nations is supposed to help people in this world who need help,' he told me with tears rolling down his face. 'Well, we eat trees. We are people. Why doesn't the UN help *us*?' I didn't have an answer for him; and selfishly, all I could think about was for him to stop crying, for I don't like to have my life in the hands of a crying guerrilla, especially if he only has one.

There were many crying guerrillas the day I reached their jungle headquarters. Hundreds of battered people, mostly unarmed civilians, greeted me with tears and cries for help. 'We are starving,' screamed one woman before she pounded herself in the chest and fell to the ground in frightening anguish. 'The Vietnamese killed my parents … I am starving,' she cried. An elderly woman next to her was clasping her hands against her face in a prayer-like gesture, begging for mercy as if I was the envoy of her salvation. The entire community, close to 2,000 tormented souls, converged on me, many of them prostrating themselves in front of me. Their clothes were torn, their bodies bruised, their hearts shattered. They were holding on to the edge of life, waiting for their jungle hell to end. One woman had an eight-inch open flesh wound on her shin that was festering. One young man had an open shrapnel wound above his eye, while another woman had part of her face missing from a B-40 rocket. There was simply no one who was devoid of grief among this hopeless rabble. The people were trapped in a living nightmare.

One member of this wretched community was a man named Nhia Tho Vang. He was one of the first to greet me along the riverbank just before we arrived at the camp. He hugged me and started to cry, speaking in Vietnamese as he was earlier informed that I could converse in that language. Nhia fled to the jungle in 1978 with four of his family members to escape retribution from the communists. His crime was that some of his relatives had fought in the CIA's secret army. Out of the group of five with whom he fled, only he was left. The others were either dead or in prison. Since we both could speak Vietnamese, Nhia became my main communication link with the community.

Their jungle settlement straddled both sides of a shallow mountain creek. The picturesque scenery was no reflection of their bleak existence. They lived in shelters similar to the ones that my escort team erected every night. Nothing in the settlement was permanent, for they had to be ready to pick up and move at any time according to the movements of government soldiers that tracked them down. By the time I arrived in mid April, they had already moved settlements ten times that year and they would move two more times during the next two and half weeks I was with them.

Out of the 2,000 people, only a hundred or so were armed. Most of their weapons were the same ones they had when they fled to the jungle in the 1970s. Ammunition was sparse and was often too old to work. Their biggest weapon was a hand-held grenade launcher, and many of the guerrillas, like Moua Thoua Ther, only had a rifle. For those who still had a uniform, most were threadbare from years of use. The only resemblance they bore to an army was seen in their discipline and their courage. Round the clock patrols and sentries were in place to guard their community and monitor enemy troop movement. Most impressive to me was their ability to fashion booby traps out of grenades and bamboo, complete with trip wires made out of jungle vine. You didn't want to be a Hmong guerrilla, but you didn't want to be their enemy either.

The majority of the community were women, children and elderly persons who shared one thing in common: they were the relatives of soldiers who fought in the CIA's secret army during the 1960s and 70s. Hundreds of people in the group had spent their entire lives on the run in the jungle. While the majority of them were Hmong, there was a small contingent of ethnic Khmu, an indigenous highland minority group from northern Laos that also contributed significant manpower to the CIA's secret army during the war. There were no schools, no clinics, or any other establishments associated with a functioning society. Life was just a struggle to survive another day, and often that was an impossible task.

I was astonished that they had absolutely no medicine. When someone saw me open my small survival kit, which had various kinds of drugs inside including antibiotics, I suddenly became the camp's doctor. People were lining up to see if I could treat their illnesses or injuries. One man was complaining of a stomachache, so I asked him how many days he had had it for. 'Oh, many years,' was his reply. I think

I gave him a Pepto-Bismal and a multivitamin; he was very grateful.

Over the course of the next few days, I attempted to treat everything from headaches to shrapnel wounds. With a limited supply of medicine, I gave the antibiotics to those I thought could benefit the most; everyone else was simply given vitamins, and I hoped that the placebo effect wasn't a phenomenon peculiar to the Western psyche. I asked Ly if there were any medics among the community, thinking that there must be at least one who trained as a medic during the war.

'Yes, we have one medic,' he confirmed. 'But he ran out of medicine in 1975.' He said it was too dangerous to send people to villages to get supplies such as medicine now, so instead they relied on traditional medicines and jungle herbs. Unfortunately, these did little to treat war wounds. I was told that 195 people in their community had died between January and April of that year, 179 from enemy attacks and 16 from illness.

'We are surrounded by 6,000 enemy troops,' the leader of the community, Yang Thua Thao, told me on my arrival during a military briefing in a jungle hut. He pinned up an old American military map of the area and pointed to enemy positions. He even gave me their coordinates. He was a disciplined soldier and an authoritative leader, although his short height and spectacles made him an unlikely warrior.

When Vang Pao disbanded the Hmong army and fled to Thailand in May 1975, Yang was on an operation along the Ho Chi Minh Trail near the Vietnamese border. He had to walk for several weeks to get back to their previous headquarters at Long Chieng, only to find, on getting there, that it was abandoned. He then tried to escape to Thailand like his commander Vang Pao, but was stopped by heavy fighting. He retreated into the jungles of Xieng Khouang with 2,000 others, where he remained. He'd been wounded seven times and I could tell he held a grudge against his former American allies. 'We used to be soldiers for America, to help fight the North Vietnamese Army and Pathet Lao,' he explained to me. 'When America left, we had nowhere to go, so we fled into the forest. We have been fighting ever since and nobody knows.' Having kept his rank since 1975, Yang Thua Thao was still a proud lieutenant.

I was astounded during the military briefing when the lieutenant asked me, in an almost demanding tone, to phone the US President George W Bush and arrange for an American air rescue operation to get his people out of Laos. Both Yang Thua Thao and Moua Thoua Ther had satellite telephones, which had been smuggled into them by the network of blackbirds. So the guerrilla leaders expected me to use one of their phones to dial a direct line to the president of the United States. The mood suddenly turned tense as I tried to explain to them that there was no way I could do that. Yang and the others could not grasp the concept that I did not have the power to phone the president and ask for an evacuation.

'I am a journalist, I do not work for the US government,' I told them. 'I can help you by taking video and pictures of your situation to show to the outside world, so that people can see your plight. When I leave, I will contact the United Nations and tell them of your desperate situation. Surely they will help.' I honestly believed what I told them, but my words were not enough. They wanted me to get them out, now.

While I didn't know it at the time, some Hmong-Americans (not associated with TJ and the blackbird network) were advising Yang Thua Thao and Moua Thoua Ther through phone conversations to hold me hostage until a UN or US evacuation flight could be organized. What I did know at the time was that Yang Thua Thao and Moua Thoua Ther were dead serious about using me to get them out—and they repeatedly insisted I call either the White House or the United Nations to arrange for an evacuation flight. They even gave me their coordinates and suggested that the plane land at Lima Site 238, the old CIA airstrip nearby. I was never threatened or mistreated in any way; on the contrary, I was well taken care of and treated as a friend. But it was clear they wanted me to help get them out. They were desperate people, and I was their lifeline. Yang told me that I might be with them for a while, and he even offered me a wife. 'And if you get us out of here', he promised, 'I'll give you three.' Needless to say, I'm still single.

After going into several war zones and following soldiers and guerrillas into battle on many occasions, I honestly thought I had pushed my luck this time with the Hmong. I was scared. While I was not afraid of the people, I was afraid that their desperate situation would lead to desperate actions that would get us captured or killed by the Laotian military.

Unsure of my situation, I simply made the best of it and concentrated on the task of documenting the lives of these people. I filmed their existence and took snapshots of their hell. I interviewed soldiers like Nhia Lo Vang, who stepped on a landmine in 1997 and made a prosthetic limb out of a tree. He had shoulder-length hair and a smile that seemed to belie his fate. In the late 1970s he was one of the resistors at Phu Bia Mountain, but now he was just resisting death. He had a gentle look about him and I took him to be a kind man. Over the following weeks, he would frequently invite me to his shelter for a meal. He even offered me his daughter for marriage, but the last thing I wanted was to complicate my already precarious situation. Besides, it was difficult to be romantic in that bleak place.

Another man I interviewed was Xong Xer Yang, the oldest man in the community. At the age of 89, he was a veteran of both the American and French wars in Indochina. 'I was a soldier for the French, but they left,' he lamented. 'Then I was a soldier for America, but they left too. Now there is no country that will help us.'

He was extremely frail and barely clinging to life; he told me he was preparing for death. Miraculously, his 80-year-old wife was also still alive, as if they could not depart this life without each other. There was another couple that seemed to share a similar destiny: a 72-year-old man named Yong Pao Yang who fought for the US from 1961 to 1975 and his ageing wife who loyally followed him throughout the years. They were a living endorsement for the institution of marriage, and there was something sweet in their bitter existence. They were a match made in hell.

One person who wasn't so fortunate however was Mai Lor. After 28 years in the jungle, his wife took a machete and stabbed herself to death. It was her only way out.

While the older ones had already beaten the odds to make it as far as they had, it was the children who had the odds stacked against them. Ten of them had already died in the first four months of the year before I arrived, and many of them showed severe signs of malnutrition and starvation. Skin rash was common and, without medicine to fight off infection, the smallest problems could turn into serious ailments. One poor boy had a severely swollen eye, which had been so for six months. To make matters worse for this six-year-old, his teeth were falling out. Nobody knew why.

For the children of this community, hide-and-seek wasn't a game, it was a way of life. There were no schools to teach the children how to read, write or do maths; the only lessons these children learned were how to survive. There was one family whose head of the shelterhold was only 13 years old. Ze Yang had been looking after his two younger brothers and one younger sister since July 2002 after a Laotian mortar round interrupted their dinner—smashing into their jungle shelter and killing both of the parents. Here, boys turned into men very quickly, and most were already carrying a weapon by the age of 12. By the age of 14, most were combat veterans. There was little time for play, and even less time for growing up.

Like everywhere else in the world, the children here were curious, and my being with them was certainly a highlight for many of them. Every day, some groups of children would come by my shelter to look at me, but often they would run away as soon as I smiled or tried to talk to them, especially the girls. One exception was a young girl of about eight, who would wait for me to wake up every morning and then make me a fire as soon as I got out of my hammock. She would even boil water for me to make my coffee. It was so cute and something that will be forever ingrained in my memory; especially when she hurriedly told me something that I could not understand and then ran off, only to return a few minutes later with a tea pot. It was as if she had said, 'Don't go anywhere, I'll be right back with a tea pot and boil you some water.'

Another lasting memory is the beautiful smile of a young woman who was probably around 16. She had a look that could brighten anyone's day. She always covered her hair in a Hmong cloth and you could tell she tried to keep herself pretty despite her ugly situation. Perhaps that was the only way she knew how to hold on to her dignity. Sadly, about three weeks after I left, while searching for food in the forest, she was ambushed by Lao soldiers. She was raped, stabbed, shot, disfigured and murdered. I prefer to remember her smile.

I had only been with the community for five days when the guerrillas received intelligence that indicated government troops were moving in on our position. This forced us to abandon camp and move on to a new location. Within hours, the entire community had packed their meager belongings, strapped them to their backs in torn bags and bamboo baskets, and filed out into the jungle in search of a new place to live. Many walked barefoot, others in flip-flops, while the lucky few had torn shoes. Boys as young as eight carried weapons, girls carried everything from babies to crossbows, and adults carried their entire possessions. The burden of misery and disinheritance, however, was something they all carried alike.

While Yang Thua Thao led his people through the forest to look for a site to make their next settlement, Moua Thoua Ther led about 12 guerrillas and me in another direction: straight towards an enemy outpost. They wanted me to film the camp to prove to the world that the Laotian government was still waging war against them.

Armed with assault rifles and a grenade launcher, we walked for about three hours until we reached a deserted village in the forest. The makeshift village was actually their own—they had lived in it the previous November and December. Being so close to enemy positions, the guerrillas first secured the area before we camped down for the night. They boobytrapped the path so that if an enemy patrol came through during the night, the explosion from the trap would wake us in time for us to flee. The device they made was ingenious. A trap was rigged so that an M-79 grenade at the bottom of a hollow piece of bamboo would explode if a piece of jungle vine was tripped; this would in turn trigger a piece of wood to strike the bamboo and the grenade. Despite this elaborate set-up, I still hoped that the Laotian soldiers, like us, only wanted to sleep that night.

After an uneventful night during which the booby trap had thankfully been left intact, we ventured closer to enemy positions, reaching a mountaintop clearing in the midafternoon. From this vantage point, a series of huts could be made out in the distance, several kilometers away along a jungle ridge. The scenery was stunning, but this was no time to marvel in the beauty of our surroundings; in the valley below us, four of Moua Thoua Ther's men fired three rounds from their grenade launcher and sprayed bullets at one of the outposts, sparking a barrage of return fire that echoed throughout the valley. The only substance to the video I captured was the thundering sound of heavy machinegun fire and mortar rounds exploding in the distance fired by government forces. But as far as the guerrillas were concerned, their mission was accomplished. Their unknown war was finally captured on video for the world to see. Little did they know that the world just didn't care.

The next day, we began the trek back to reach the rest of the community who were camped on a hillside two day's walk away. We were descending a steep mountain gorge when we were suddenly hit by a torrential downpour. Drenched, freezing, and dangerously negotiating the slick rocks of the canyon, I remember thinking that even nature herself seems determined to thwart the unfortunate Hmong. Without houses, proper clothing, and medicine, the elements can be just as dangerous as enemy fire. While I could derive comfort from the fact that my misery was temporary, I knew that the guerrillas did not have that luxury. Their misery was permanent; it was their life. There was no light at the end of the tunnel or a promise of a better future for them. Their future, like their present, was as dark as the sky above the gorge.

That afternoon, as the guerrillas erected rudimentary shelters for the night, soaking and shivering in the rain, Nhia Tho Vang, the Vietnamese-speaking guerrilla, turned to me and spoke on the verge of tears, 'We don't like to live like this,' he said apologetically, as if asking me to excuse their misery. 'But America left us and Vang Pao left us and we can't live under the communists ... so we have to live like this, we have no other choice.' We fell asleep that evening to the sound of drizzling rain and the promise of a wet, uncomfortable night.

After another day's walk, we met up with the rest of the community who were living on a jungle hillside. The scene of the new camp was a mosaic of life and survival: children were peeling bamboo shoots to prepare for mealtime; women were boiling water and preparing whatever root, plant or edible species that they would call dinner that night; two boys were preparing their crossbows to hunt for small game; Nhia Lo Vang, the one-legged guerrilla, was resting under his lean-to, still recovering from the difficult journey of the previous days carrying several kilos on his back plus his AK-47 (he may have had a leg missing, but you could hardly call him handicapped); and Ly Dang, the veteran guerrilla who spent eight years in the Laotian gulag, was trying to treat his feverish son with traditional jungle medicine, but to little avail. The hillside that day was home to nearly 2,000 people trying to overcome the challenges of daily life. The next day it was a deserted slope as empty as the lives of the people who left it as they moved on in their never-ending journey of life on the run.

There were brilliant pictures to be taken that day as I trekked through the forest with 2,000 people on the move. Unfortunately, I only got a few. It's hard to take pictures when you are also the subject—experiencing the same hardship, pain and misery of the people you are supposed to be documenting. I saw many great pictures, but most of the time I was too exhausted to stop and take them, or by the time I had my eye through the viewfinder the image was gone. One was of a boy about eight years old carrying a World War Two carbine in one hand and an American-issued Vietnam War army canteen in the other—the photo caption would have read, 'Eight-year-old with World War Two rifle still fighting the Vietnam War.' There were teenage girls carrying AK-47 assault rifles and Nhia Lo Vang was hobbling along on one leg with the help of a tree stump for a foot and a bamboo cane that somehow stayed out of the way of his AK-47. The stronger members of the group would double back and help carry the loads of the people who were struggling. While I managed to get a few powerful images on film that day, most of the pictures I took could only be developed in the darkroom of my mind.

During that day we were met by four guerrillas from a separate community who had walked for three days to say hello. They were eager to see me and explain their plight, 'We have it worse,' one of the newcomers told me, as if it was a competition for grief. 'We have more people who are sick. The enemy attacks us *every* day', he insisted. He asked me if I would like to visit their group, but I politely declined, not wanting to walk an extra six days. They couldn't have been with us for more than an hour before they said goodbye and began their three-day journey back, but not before Yang Thua Thao gave them his pistol and a handful of bullets. Perhaps they really were worse off.

The group's new home was on the banks of a muddy creek that quietly coursed its way through the forest. The abundance of bamboo shoots in the area was a welcome source of food for the community, and one man even killed a squirrel which allowed a lucky few to get a dose of protein. Even though the Hmong are renowned as hunters, this community was unable to reap the benefits of their traditional trade because of three major problems: the shortage of bullets, which meant they could only use them sparingly; the fact that any shot they did fire could give their position away to nearby government soldiers; and the fact that their hunting territory was extremely limited due to the heavy presence of government soldiers in their surrounding area. Indeed, hunting, for them, was a risky activity in which they could easily go from being predator to prey.

While the restrictions on hunting adversely affected their diet, it was their inability to cultivate rice which caused the greatest grievance. Traditionally the Hmong have practiced slash-and-burn agriculture, clearing and burning mountain slopes to grow crops such as rice and corn using the ashes from the clearing process as fertilizer. When the soil became depleted after a few years, villages were abandoned and relocated. For this community, and other similar groups scattered throughout northern Laos, stepped up government campaigns against them since 1999 made it impossible for them to stay in one place long enough to cultivate crops. Their traditional slash-and-burn agriculture was replaced by digging and scavenging. 'We are the same as animals in the forest,' Ly, the English-speaking guerrilla told me, explaining that they hadn't been able to grow rice since 2000. 'We live just like them.'

In December 1999, the Laotian government stepped up its military campaign to defeat the last of the Hmong resistance, which by that time represented very little threat to the government or to the security of the communist state. A key aspect of this new campaign involved thwarting the Hmong's ability to grow rice and depriving them of many of their other food sources. It's a common counter-insurgency tactic that the Laotian government did remarkably well. Reports began to trickle out of Laos of the worsening conditions, but most of them only reached Hmong communities overseas and never made the headlines of the international media. One such report occurred in the spring of 2000, when TJ returned from a clandestine trip to Laos and reported to General Vang Pao in California of the situation.

Alarmed at such reports and ashamed at their government's betrayal of the Hmong in Laos, an American couple who were friends with TJ, Ed and Georgie Szendrey, along with another Hmong-American named Ger Vang decided to do something about it. With the support of General Vang Pao, the group made a fact-finding trip to Thailand and to the Thai-Lao border in December 2001 where they conducted over 30 hours of interviews. Those interviewed included guerrilla leaders, who clandestinely crossed the border to see them, some villagers, Hmong refugees in Thailand and three former Lao government soldiers. A satellite phone was given to one of the jungle leaders and some video cameras were also dispersed to the various groups. Upon their return to the States, the group founded the Fact Finding Commission (FFC), a small organization aimed at raising awareness of the plight of the Hmong and other groups of secret veterans of the US war still fighting in the jungles of Laos. With TJ forming the blackbird network, more satellite phones were smuggled into the groups, which enabled semi-regular communication between them, the FFC and other Hmong-Americans. Using solar panels that were also smuggled in to them, phone and video batteries could be recharged, which, in more ways than one, gave the guerrillas and their family members a new source of power.

By the time I had settled in with Moua Thoua Ther's group at their third camp in three weeks at the end of April 2004, all I wanted to do was leave. As a journalist, my work with them was finished. I had the pictures, the video, and the information I needed to tell their story, along with the extraordinary experience of having met and lived among this forgotten people trapped in a time warp of the Vietnam War. I had entered their nightmare and lived it with them. Now it was time to exit, but many elders of the community, including the commander Yang Thua Thao, didn't want to open the door to my departure. For five long days, I waited anxiously to leave as the group's leaders contemplated what to do with me: should they keep me as a hostage to try and force an international rescue operation, or should they release me and hope that my video, pictures and messages would be enough to spark an international response to save them? I tried desperately to convince them that the latter option was the only viable choice, and that the only way I could help them was for them to let me leave and take their case to the United Nations. I promised that, as soon as I was escorted out of the jungle and I reached the safety of Thailand, that was exactly what I would do. In my naivety, I honestly believed the words that I told them, 'The United Nations *has* to help you—that's what the UN is for, to help people like you.' I couldn't have been more wrong.

While I was desperately negotiating with the leaders of the community to let me go, TJ and the FFC were frantically urging them, through satellite phone communication, to release me, explaining to them that holding me hostage would have severe negative implications. TJ even relayed to them that it was a direct order of General Vang Pao to release me.

In the end, the guerrilla leaders settled for a phone call. They would arrange for my departure from the jungle so long as I called the Bangkok office of the United Nations High Commissioner for Refugees (UNHCR), explaining the Hmong's dire situation and relaying their demands to be rescued. I agreed. I still feel sorry for the poor woman at the UNHCR office who picked up my call.

'Hi, I am a journalist currently with a group of nearly 2,000 ex-CIA soldiers and their family members in northern Laos who are demanding that they be rescued and receive refugee status.' Although I half thought she would hang up in the belief that it was a prank call, she handled the call remarkably well. 'Let me get this straight, you are with 2,000 Hmong right now in Laos who want to become refugees?'

'Yes,' I replied. 'They are former CIA soldiers and their family members who never surrendered in 1975. They are making me call you to tell you that they want to be rescued.'

Knowing there was absolutely nothing she could do, I told her I would provide her with more details in person as soon as I arrived in Thailand. I also asked her to keep the phone call to herself until then, for the last thing I wanted was for her to start making phone calls to Lao authorities. She promised that she would, asked if I was all right and, before hanging up, she told me in a motherly manner to take care.

While the phone call was enough to satisfy the leaders of the community, I often wonder if they made the right choice in letting me leave. Would more lives have been saved in the long run if such a hostage drama had been played out in the jungles of Laos? Should I have conspired with them? These are questions I can contemplate with the luxury of hindsight, but at the time they were not even possibilities. The instinct for survival can often reduce us to be most selfish.

Finally, on the morning of 30 April, Moua Thoua Ther and eight of his soldiers led me out of their camp to begin the three day journey back to the dirt road where I had been dropped off by my blackbird nearly three weeks before. While I was thrilled to be leaving, many people in the community were in tears, as if they were watching their lifeline to the outside world slip away into the forest. Some even started following us, forcing Moua Thoua Ther to order them to stay put in the camp. One young Khmu man grabbed me and burst into tears, begging me to save them and not forget them. It's hard to console someone who lives in the pit of despair and who needs a miracle just to start the climb back out. I can't recall what I told him, but it probably just gave him a false sense of hope. When you're in a hopeless situation, I guess false hope is better than none.

After a four-hour walk, we set up camp that night on a small jungle hillside. For the first time in three weeks I was excited because I knew I was on my way out. I allowed my mind to drift forward to what awaited: bitter roots would be replaced by cheeseburgers and pizzas; boiled water by Coke and cold beer. I thought about crossing the Mekong River back to Thailand, and how happy I would be arriving on the other side. I knew of the dangers that still lay ahead. There was still the threat of army patrols, or of being searched at immigration in possession of video of a war that the government denied existed. But I preferred to ignore them and put my trust in fate, confident that all would turn out well. However, on the third day of our journey out, those dangers became very apparent as Laotian soldiers zeroed in on our position.

With plenty of ground to cover on the third and final day of our journey out, we awoke before dawn and began the day's trek in the early morning darkness. A drizzling rain fell with the first light of the morning, and dealt its dreariness as we pushed on toward the jungle's edge. Attempting to keep my newfound optimism, I thought to myself that perhaps the rain was a good thing—maybe it would deter government soldiers from patrolling the area. I didn't know it at the time, but I was right. The rain may have actually saved my life that morning for we walked straight into an enemy position where 20 government soldiers were holed up in their outpost to keep dry from the rain. The point man in our group didn't see the bamboo structure that sheltered the soldiers until he had almost walked past it, potentially exposing us to target practice as we rounded a bend straight into their site. I remember seeing the outpost on my right, about a hundred meters away, then looking back and seeing the soldier behind me signaling back to the rest of the group to alert them. I was in the middle of our column, frantically looking both ways to see what to do.

A soldier in front of me aimed his weapon at the hut and headed straight to it, ready to unload his magazine as the rest of us hit the ground for cover, before we crawled back in the direction we had come from. Even if I had my video camera in hand, I don't know if I would have had the presence of mind to start filming, but it would have made an awesome sequence: the hut, the soldier signaling, the brave guerrilla ready to unleash his payload, the rest of the group hitting the ground, the expressions of shock and fear ... but once again I could only capture the pictures in my head.

Before long, our crawl turned into an all-out sprint for cover in the nearby trees. Using their decades of experience (between the nine of them they probably had over 250 years of soldiering experience), they ran one way to purposely leave a trail that could easily be followed by enemy troops in pursuit, then turned back and individually went off the trail in another direction to conceal our movement. The ten of us spread out and climbed a jungle slope in various directions in order to avoid making a single, easy-to-follow trail, before converging and regrouping at the top of the hill.

During this frantic escape, I initially thought the outpost was deserted, for that was the only logical reason I could think of for why they didn't fire on us. Then, after some of the guerrillas insisted the outpost was manned, I thought maybe there were only one or two soldiers manning it and they didn't want to engage in a gun battle in which they were considerably outnumbered. It wasn't until we regrouped at the top of the hill that I learned the outpost was actually fully manned. The brave guerrilla who walked towards the outpost ready to unleash his firepower said he saw about 20 soldiers manning the position. He only turned back when he realized that we hadn't been spotted. The guerrillas explained to me that because it was raining the soldiers were sheltering to keep dry, leaving their position unguarded. My optimism about the rain proved right, but I still welcomed the sun when it broke through the clouds and reinvigorated our dampened mood.

It was a nerve-wracking morning as we continued to push on, constantly alert to see if there were any soldiers in pursuit. I certainly didn't want to be caught in a gun battle alongside rebels who were considerably outnumbered and whose only real defence tactic is to run. My main concern, besides getting killed, was being forced to turn back. Ly, the English-speaking guerrilla, did little to reassure me of the situation. He told me point blank, 'If the enemy attacks us, just start running and try to make your own way out of the jungle.' He said it so casually and calmly as if he was reaffirming a plan that I should have already known, but it made me feel anything but calm, and if it was a plan, I sure as hell didn't like it. I decided that if it came down to it, I'd go with Plan B: anything but Ly's plan.

As we got farther from the outpost and closer to the jungle's edge, the dreaded thought of those plans slowly faded into the back of my mind, and were of little concern by the time we stopped for a rest in the forest just before dusk. As we rested and prepared for the final few kilometers of the journey, Moua Thoua Ther took out a candle and asked one of his men for a light. Thinking he was lighting the candle to use as a flashlight for the coming darkness, my spirits were immediately rejuvenated as I knew we could only use a light if we were out of enemy range, otherwise the flickering in the darkness could give us away. But my flame of hope was soon extinguished when Ly explained the real purpose of lighting the candle; it was a vigil for the spirits to protect us in the night. Moua Thoua Ther said a few prayers and then placed the candle on the ground before venturing off into the night. We weren't out of enemy range after all.

The vigil was working. By 8pm the ten of us were waiting in the bushes just off the trail in the vicinity where Moua Thoua Ther's men had met me 21 days before. Thirty minutes before, they had phoned the blackbird—Number 32—to tell him we had arrived and that everything was set for the pick up. Now, all we had to do was wait. The next few hours were some of the longest in my life as I sat anxiously awaiting Number 32's arrival. My senses were strained for any indication of his approach. While I waited, I dreaded the thought of Number 32 not showing up, or any other scenario in which my exit from the jungle would be prevented or even delayed. As minutes turned into hours, my anxiety multiplied. Once again I found myself in constant prayer, just like 21 days before when I was in the back of the stalled car that eventually brought me here. I guess you could say my prayers were answered at 11:30pm when Number 32 finally emerged; but I like to think it was the spirits solicited by the candle.

While happiness consumed me, a part of me was sad to say goodbye to Moua Thoua Ther, See Xeng Ly, Va Char Yang, Ly Dang and the others who had allowed me to enter their nightmare and guided me safely through it. I knew I would probably never see them again, and that this jungle, which provided them with everything they needed, would probably provide them with their graves as well. I emptied my backpack and gave them almost all of my belongings, everything from a life-changing sleeping bag to a mundane plastic container. They were overjoyed. That night I was saying goodbye to anonymous heroes whose reward for loyalty and bravery had been abandonment and suffering. While I was determined to tell their story and take their plight to the United Nations, I couldn't help but think that perhaps I too was abandoning them. As I followed Number 32 into the darkness, leaving Moua Thoua Ther and his men to the mercy of the night, I didn't dare look back.

After an hour's walk, we arrived in a small village where I was sheltered in a farmhouse until just before dawn. I was given some food before falling asleep on a hard-wooded bed, my first bed in over three weeks. At 5am, we left the house in Number 32's beat-up old car to drive back to Phonsavan. He instructed me to lie down in the back and pretend to be asleep as we drove out of the restricted Xaysomboune area. I did as he said and lay down in the back, closed my eyes, and tried not to think about the consequences of getting stopped at a checkpoint. It was Phonsavan or bust.

We arrived without any problems just after daybreak, leaving nine hours to kill before the day's only bus left for the capital Vientiane. I knew I had to lay low and not draw the attention of the authorities in the town; it was quite possible that they knew a journalist was on the way out of Xaysomboune. I spent most of the day in the back of a restaurant sipping beer and revelling in my first good meal in weeks while anxiously waiting for the bus's departure at 3pm. The plan was that Number 32 would accompany me on the trip to Vientiane, although we would buy our tickets separately and not sit beside each other. He would take my bag just in case I was searched at one of the many checkpoints on the way out of the city and province. I didn't really like the plan, especially since there was nothing I had that would indicate I had just spent three weeks with the Hmong except for my undeveloped film and videotapes (which the authorities wouldn't know what was on them unless they developed the film or forced me to play the videotapes on my camera), but I decided to trust his judgment. There was no way I was going to relinquish my film and videotapes so I kept them in the pockets of my vest, wearing it at all times. I thought it might draw suspicion if I was searched on the bus and didn't have a bag, so I went to the market and bought a small backpack and some items to put inside it.

According to plan, I met Number 32 at a pre-arranged meeting place in town at 2pm to give him my bag, and met him again at the station just before 3pm. Ignoring each other, we boarded the bus separately for the 11-hour ride to Vientiane. He was carrying my bag and camera gear while I carried my small new backpack, wearing my vest full of film and videotapes. I felt like a criminal, as if I was carrying a vest full of narcotics. It was going to be a long ride, but it sure as hell beat walking. I never asked Number 32 what would happen if the authorities searched him.

After we passed through the first checkpoint, I sat back and began to relax. As we meandered through the mountains of Xieng Khouang, I stared out the window and marvelled at the lush green scenery that spanned off into the distance. It was hard to believe that I had just returned from somewhere out in those mountains, and that such a beautiful place could be a cauldron of such suffering and despair. I thought of Moua Thoua Ther and the guerrillas I had left the night before and of how they were coping today, and what awaited them in the future. Knowing they were hiding somewhere in that endless jungle that spread out before my eyes, I gazed out the window and wished them well.

We arrived in Vientiane in the early morning hours. In the safety and anonymity of the capital, Number 32 and I refrained from our feigned disassociation with each other and grabbed a *tuk-tuk* to a hotel, checking into two separate rooms. I had my first shower in almost a month before falling fast asleep in the wonderful softness of a bed and a pillow. The dingy hotel was my Shangri-La and I had the best sleep I had had in weeks.

The next morning, I said goodbye to Number 32 and headed to the border for the final hurdle of my trip—to exit Laos and return to Thailand. After all I had been through in the past month I dreaded the thought of making it this far only to be caught at the border by Laotian immigration. I was nervous. Fortunately, the Laotian immigration officer could not hear the pounding of my heart as I gave her my passport. All the time I was desperately hoping she would not ask me any questions or search my belongings. She was the only thing standing in the way of my freedom and journalistic accomplishment of documenting the Hmong's secret war. I gave her my passport and flashed a half smile to come across as pleasant but avoided seeming overly friendly. I briefly looked her in the eye, and casually waited for her permission to leave. I will never forget the sound of her stamp hitting down on my passport, leaving a beautiful mark on both my passport and my life. When I crossed into Thailand shortly afterwards, tears of joy filled my eyes and rolled down my face. The dark clouds had passed and the sun was shining, while a serene calmness filled the air. My ordeal had ended.

Immediately after arriving in Thailand I consulted the FFC on the appropriate course of action to take to help the Hmong and to deliver their messages to the UN as I had promised. Within a few days, I boarded a flight to the US courtesy of the FFC where I spent much of the next month meeting with Hmong-American leaders and community members as well as traveling to New York and Washington DC to meet with UN and US government officials. I was joined by filmmakers Ruhi Hamid and Misha Maltsev who also recently returned from the jungles of Laos on assignment with the BBC to document the Hmong's secret war. Bound by our life-changing experiences with the Hmong, we immediately became good friends and tried our best to keep our promises to the people we had visited in the jungle who wanted nothing except to be rescued. They didn't want to fight any more but feared that surrender would be a death sentence. Indeed, after almost half a century at war with the Laotian communists, the Hmong have learned never to trust their life-long enemy, and for good reason—too many of their family members, friends, and comrades have met their deaths at their hands, have been sentenced to lengthy prison terms, or have simply vanished. Surrender, for many of them, is simply not an option.

Backed by both the FFC and Amnesty International, Ruhi and I briefed a United Nations Panel in New York in early June 2004 on the plight of the Hmong and delivered their pleas for help. While the group that Ruhi and Misha visited were in a different province of Laos, Borikhamsay, the condition of the people was equally miserable and their leaders asked the same of Ruhi and Misha as Yang Thua Thao and Moua Thoua Ther had asked of me: for salvation. What these leaders wanted, and what Ruhi and I relayed to the UN, was to surrender under the eyes of international monitors to guarantee their safety. For an army that was abandoned and forgotten and a people whose plight has been ignored by the outside world, it wasn't much to ask. They weren't asking for support, they weren't asking for compensation—they weren't even asking for recognition. All they wanted was to be saved. While the UN officials we briefed expressed tremendous interest and sympathy in the matter, the bottom line is that the world's largest organization has done nothing to help these people. Neither has the United States government, which is directly responsible for this tragedy. During a meeting with US State Department officials in Washington shortly afterwards, a senior officer asked me if the Hmong in the jungle were aware of Washington's policy of no longer supporting anti-communist resistance groups in Southeast Asia.

'Yes,' I replied, 'they are fully aware of this policy. That is why they are dying.

'They are not asking for support,' I continued. 'They are asking to be saved.'

After no response from the UN, the US government, or the international community, the Hmong have had no other choice but to help themselves. In June 2005, with the advice, consultation and assistance of the FFC, 173 people, mostly women, children, and elderly persons from Moua Thoua Ther's group walked out of the jungle and surrendered to the government, believing in two things: that they would not survive another rainy season in the jungle if they stayed, and that the international community would assure their safety if they surrendered. While they may have been right on the first belief, they couldn't have been more wrong on the second.

Despite forewarning and a valiant campaign by the FFC to notify various UN and relief groups and members of the diplomatic community in Vientiane and Bangkok, including US embassy officials, the only ones to meet the 173 battered and emaciated people on 4 June 2005 in the village of Chong Thuang in Xieng Khouang province were Ed and Georgie Szendrey of the FFC. The couple, along with their Hmong-American translator, Nhia Vang Yang, spent the next two nights in a Laotian jail before being deported for illegally liaising with the Hmong. Their driver, Sia Cher Vang, also a Hmong-American, was arrested as well and held for several days. As for the 173 people who surrendered in the belief that their safety would be guaranteed by the international community, they were loaded into four military trucks at gunpoint and driven to an army camp outside the town of Phou Kout. They then spent the next six months in custody, the first two confined in holding cells. Not one international organization, relief agency or NGO was given access to them. Several of them escaped and ended up in prison in Thailand as illegal immigrants. Occasionally I pay them a visit but every time I do so I feel ashamed to be a member of the human race. As a collective, we have failed people like the Hmong.

At the time of writing, the tragic story of the Hmong continues to unfold. When I visited Moua Thoua Ther and Yang Thua Thao's group in April 2004, they told me that 17,669 of them were still holding out in the jungles of Laos. By the end of 2007, the FFC estimated there to be only about 4,000 left—the rest had either surrendered, escaped to Thailand, or had perished. Moua Thoua Ther escaped to Thailand sometime in 2007 where he remained in hiding in 2008. Yang Thua Thao was not as fortunate. He was ambushed and killed in March 2007, dying in battle nearly 32 years after the war for which he was recruited to fight officially ended. I guess his time had finally come.

In one last betrayal of the Hmong, General Vang Pao and ten of his associates were arrested in June 2007 in California, accused of trying to purchase 9.8

million dollars worth of weapons and ammunition to overthrow the Lao government. If he's found guilty, Vang Pao faces life imprisonment. While the United Nations, US government and the international community have turned their backs on the Hmong, the only group that has refused to do the same now faces life in prison. The irony disturbs me.

The Hmong were not the only ones betrayed and forgotten by the United States at the end of the Vietnam War. In the early 1960s, at the same time the CIA was recruiting the Hmong for its clandestine war in Laos, the agency was also recruiting tribesmen in the Central Highlands of South Vietnam in order to prevent Vietnamese communist forces from gaining control of the area. In conjunction with US Special Forces, the CIA armed and trained these tribesmen, collectively referred to as Montagnards (French for 'mountain people') to form village defense units throughout the Central Highlands. The Montagnards were also recruited and trained to conduct reconnaissance and paramilitary operations. They operated alongside US Special Forces and quickly earned a legendary reputation as some of the most loyal and brave fighters of the war. At any given time during the war, an estimated 40,000 Montagnards were serving alongside US forces, providing the backbone of counter-insurgency efforts in the strategic Central Highlands. This was the region often cited as the place where the war would be won or lost.

Like the Hmong, several thousand Montagnards were also recruited into communist forces during the war, but the majority sided with the Americans as they viewed the Vietnamese as invaders of their homeland and saw the opportunity to gain autonomy from both North and South Vietnam by siding with the United States. Furthermore, conversion to Christianity by the French in the early 19th century, as well as by American missionaries in the 1930s, made the Montagnards naturally inclined to side with the US.

While eager to join forces and fight with the United States, the Montagnards also had their own political and military agenda. Unrest had been brewing in the Central Highlands of Vietnam for several years following the partition of Vietnam into North and South in 1954, and the subsequent actions of the government of South Vietnam to assume direct control over the highlands and to implement policies that would have a profoundly negative effect on the Montagnard way of life. Previously, under the French colonial government, the highlands were an autonomous region with legislation in place that guaranteed the protection of Montagnard lands and of their political rights. Before the French, the highlands were beyond the jurisdiction of Vietnamese emperors and the Montagnards were virtually left alone as they lived a semi-nomadic life as hunters and gatherers.

Under the South Vietnamese government of Ngo Dinh Diem, an estimated 850,000 ethnic Vietnamese were resettled in the Central Highlands under a land development program to relieve the demographic pressure in the South caused by the arrival of two million refugees from the North. Diem also wanted to build a 'human wall' to block a communist infiltration of the region. Tens of thousands of Montagnards were pushed off their lands into more remote areas, while repressive policies were introduced to assimilate the Montagnards into mainstream Vietnamese society.

In response to South Vietnam's repressive policies in the Central Highlands, several Montagnard leaders banded together to unite their tribes against the Vietnamese. They thus formed a resistance movement called BAJARAKA (an acronym using the first two letters of the four main tribes: Bahnar, Jarai, Rhade, and Koho). Initially their resistance was peaceful, but following a ruthless crackdown on their movement which saw the arrest, imprisonment and torture of several of their leaders, the group resorted to an armed struggle in 1964 with the formation of FULRO (a French acronym for the United Front for the Liberation of Oppressed Races). This was an armed umbrella group that united BAJARAKA with two other minority groups in neighboring Cambodia—the Champa Liberation Front and the Kampuchea Krom Liberation Front.

FULRO launched its first major operation in September 1964 when 3,000 of its soldiers, who were working with US Special Forces, revolted and took control of several villages in the highlands and killed several South Vietnamese soldiers. Sympathetic US Special Forces soldiers volunteered to be 'hostages' to serve as negotiators. A US-brokered deal was soon reached in which the rebels surrendered in return for a variety of concessions from the South Vietnamese government. Among these was the release of several of its leaders from prison. While granted amnesty, FULRO leader Y Bham Enoul fled to Cambodia with about 2,000 of his followers. This left FULRO divided into two main groups: a primarily political group based in Cambodia, and a militant group based in the Central Highlands which was working closely with US Special Forces.

As the Vietnam War heated up and the Central Highlands became a key staging ground of the war, FULRO kept in the background while many of its members fought alongside US forces, receiving arms, training and combat experience in the process. Montagnards were known for going out on operations heavily armed and returning to American base camps fully depleted of ammunition after having little or no contact with the enemy; they were stashing it for FULRO.

The war inevitably took a devastating toll on the Montagnards and on their land, destroying an estimated 85 percent of their villages and killing some 200,000 of their people—nearly four times the number of American soldiers that were killed in the war. Despite their colossal losses, in early April 1975, as communist forces were approaching Saigon and about to win the war, several Montagnard leaders met with US officials at the American Embassy in Saigon to seek guidance and support for continuing a guerrilla war against the communists. The leaders left the embassy that day with promises that the US would support them in their fight. Under the FULRO banner, about 10,000 Montagnards fled into the jungle and began a guerrilla war that would go almost unknown by the outside world for the next 17 years. Their promised support from the Americans never came.

As FULRO melted into the jungle, tens of thousands of other Montagnards were rounded up by the communist victors and sent to re-education camps as punishment for helping the Americans during the war. One such man was Sui Thom, an ethnic Jarai tribesman who fought for ten years with the US Special Forces. I met Thom in his village in Dak Lak province in the Central Highlands in 2001, and again in 2003. Like many Montagnards who fought alongside US forces during the war, he spoke fluent English with a distinct American accent (I even once met a Montagnard man who spoke with an African American accent). During one of our many conversations, Thom told me how he had been offered a place on a US evacuation flight departing from the coastal city of Nha Trang during the final days of the war in 1975. Rushing to the airport in the chaos, he arrived half an hour too late. '30 minutes,' he told me over 28 years later, shaking his head in regret. 'It drives me crazy to this day.' Instead of living a new life in America, he was given a new life in a communist re-education camp where he languished for the next six years.

While Thom was suffering in 're-education', FULRO was suffering on the battlefield. By 1977, their ammunition was running low and casualties were mounting from both enemy fire and disease. Food was also becoming scarce, and they were running out of places to hide. Their situation was so severe that they soon withdrew from Vietnam to seek sanctuary under

Pol Pot's Khmer Rouge in neighboring Mondolkiri province. By the end of the decade, over 80 percent of their original fighting force, which numbered about 10,000 soldiers, were either dead or languishing in Vietnamese prisons. Despite this, FULRO continued to launch small-scale cross-border attacks on Vietnam for more than a decade.

As FULRO was engaged in its desperate struggle, immense changes were taking place in the highlands. Shortly after the communist reunification of the country in 1975, Hanoi began launching programs to resettle large numbers of ethnic Vietnamese into the region, just as the government of South Vietnam had done in the 1950s. For their plan to establish New Economic Zones, state forestry enterprises and state rubber and coffee plantations, more than one million Vietnamese were resettled into the highlands between 1976 and 1978, while tens of thousands of Montagnards were forcibly relocated to the valleys to grow rice and industrial crops. While government-sponsored migration eased following the liberalization of the economy in 1986, voluntary migration shot up, as people wanted to take advantage of the booming coffee industry.

The influx of Vietnamese settlers into the highlands, and the government's push to develop the region, resulted in state confiscation of Montagnard lands, forced assimilation, massive deforestation, soil erosion, competition over resources, and an end to the Montagnards' customary slash-and-burn agricultural practices. By the early 1990s, the only Montagnards not affected by these changes and still living free in the forest were the rag-tag guerrillas of FULRO. However, this wouldn't be for long.

In June 1992, 17 years after 10,000 FULRO guerrillas fled into the jungle with promises of US support to continue to wage war against communist Vietnam, their forgotten army emerged from the jungles of Mondolkiri. With UN peacekeepers in the area following Vietnam's withdrawal from Cambodia, FULRO members introduced themselves to French troops at a UN cantonment site near the Vietnamese border. Amazingly (and sadly), one of their first requests was directed to the US embassy in Phnom Penh for a re-supply of weapons, ammunition and field gear. They also wanted to know what had happened to their leader, Y Bham Enoul, who they hadn't heard from since 1975. In fact, they were still awaiting orders from him. For 17 years they had fought unaware that their leader had been executed by the Khmer Rouge shortly after the group came to power in April 1975. Devastated and denied US support, the group reluctantly surrendered their weapons to UN peacekeepers and gave up their armed struggle. Their largest weapon was an M-79 grenade launcher which had one remaining round of ammunition. They were granted political asylum and resettled in the US state of North Carolina. When they left Cambodia, they vowed that one day they would return to finish their struggle.

The surrender of FULRO marked the end of the Montagnard's armed resistance against the Vietnamese, but it didn't mark the end of instability and unrest in the Central Highlands. Throughout the 1990s, land conflicts and religious repression escalated, mainly due to the continued influx of Vietnamese settlers into the region and Hanoi's communist-driven policy of keeping tight control over the population—and particularly over the Montagnards who the government still viewed with suspicion and resentment for their wartime allegiance to America, and their long history of rebellion and resistance.

By the end of the decade, the situation in the Central Highlands was as volatile as it had ever been in peacetime. Not only were the Montagnards fevered by their longstanding grievances but they were experiencing increased religious persecution and economic hardship, mainly from falling coffee prices.

In response to such grievances, an underground movement was established in 2000 in the Central Highlands with the support of the US-based Montagnard Foundation, an organization led by a Jarai-American named Kok Ksor who fought with FULRO in the 1960s and early 70s. Hundreds of Montagnards were recruited into the movement and they began holding clandestine village meetings and secretly communicating with Montagnard leaders in the US by telephone, fax and by smuggled letters and tape cassettes. Supporters began to disseminate information about the movement throughout the region which aspired towards independence through peaceful means. Several former FULRO soldiers who had been resettled in the United States returned to their home villages as tourists to help the cause.

The next year, in February 2001, the situation came to a head when the movement organized massive demonstrations and thousands of Montagnards took to the streets in the highland towns of Pleiku and Boun Me Thuot to voice their grievances. The government responded to the protests by sending in the army and paramilitary units, making a series of arrests, and sealing off the highlands to outsiders. The crackdown sent a wave of Montagnards over the border to neighboring Cambodia where they sought sanctuary and asylum. By the end of June, about 400 Montagnards were being sheltered by the UNHCR in makeshift camps in northeast Cambodia.

In April 2001, I emailed Kok Ksor and told him that I was planning a trip to the Central Highlands. I asked him if he could put me in touch with some Montagnards who I could interview about the current situation. He thanked me for my interest in his people and applauded my objective. However, he refused to put me in contact with anyone. 'I wish I could ask one of my people to speak to you,' he replied in his email. 'Unfortunately this would mean death for whomever you interview.' I chose not to push him further on the matter.

In a later communication, however, he gave me a contact name of one of the Montagnards who had recently fled from Vietnam to Cambodia and was being sheltered in a refugee camp in Mondolkiri. His name was Hoa Mai, and he was tied to Ksor's underground movement that had emerged the year before.

I arrived in Mondolkiri in late June, trying to put together a story on the Montagnards for *Soldier of Fortune* magazine. When I arrived at the refugee camp on the outskirts of the provincial capital of Senmonorom, I made the mistake of checking in with the UNHCR official who was in charge of the camp to ask him for permission to enter. When I told him I was writing a story for *Soldier of Fortune* and that I wanted to meet a refugee by the name of Hoa Mai, he refused me entry into the camp and asked me to leave. I explained to him that I had come a long way and politely asked him if it was possible to just look around, to which he replied 'no'.

I slowly walked back towards the path to leave the camp and as soon as I got out of sight of the UNHCR official, I took out my camera and started taking pictures. Within minutes, some Montagnard refugees came up to me and desperately wanted to talk. After explaining to them that I was just refused entry into the camp, they told me that the UNHCR official left the camp at the end of the day and slept in Senmonorom, so they told me to come back just after dark, at 7pm. They would wait for me at the spot where we were now. Excited, I walked back to town and waited for the dusk.

As daylight faded, I began the 30-minute walk back to the camp, following a small road before veering off into a path for the final 500 meters. As I was walking down the road, maybe a third of the way to the camp, a vehicle began approaching from the direction of the camp. Immediately recognizing it as the UNHCR's Land Cruiser, I hurried off the road into some tall grass where I pretended to relieve myself, facing opposite the road, hoping I wouldn't be recognized. After being refused entry into the camp, the last thing I wanted now was to be caught sneaking into it in the dark. The vehicle passed by without stopping and, once it was out of sight, I returned to the road and walked onwards to the camp.

Darkness descended quickly, and by the time I reached the turnoff to the camp, I was walking blindly. I walked in the general direction of the camp, convinced there was no way I was going to find my contacts in the darkness, and fearing I wouldn't even be able to find my way back to the road. But these were Montagnards—I didn't have to find them, they would find me—and they did. Out of the darkness three men appeared who were evidently happy to see me, but not as happy as I was to see them.

We sat down in the sparse forest and I began to interview them. They were anxious to tell me their stories, wanting the world, and especially America, to know their plight. All three had taken part in the protests in February 2001 and had recently fled to Cambodia in fear of their lives. Dieu Mien (not his real name as he did not want me to reveal it for security concerns) was arrested by Vietnamese police five days after he took part in the Boun Me Thuot protest on 3 February, which ended when three Vietnamese tanks rolled into the city later in the afternoon. He spent the next three months in prison where, he said, he was beaten and subjected to electric shock torture. He told me that he was only released because the police were afraid he was about to die. Believing he would be re-arrested once he regained his strength, he decided to head straight for the Cambodian border.

It wasn't the first time he crossed into Mondolkiri. In 1969, when he was just nine years old, Mien followed his father across the frontier to a FULRO camp. By the time he was 16 he was a FULRO soldier carrying on his father's struggle who had died in battle a few years before. He was eventually captured and sent to prison in 1983. When we talked that night, he didn't know what the future would hold for him, but he knew he could never return to his homeland. 'I don't know where I'll go, but I know I can't return to Vietnam. If I'm arrested and sent to prison for the third time, surely I will be executed.'

While Mien was in prison in March 2001, Y Bion was hiding in a coffee plantation. Vietnamese police were after him as well for his role in the demonstrations, but he was doing everything he could to evade capture. After two months in hiding, he also fled across the frontier to Mondolkiri. He was just a boy when the Americans left Vietnam, but he sadly still wondered if they would return to help his people.

'I am sure we could re-take the highlands,' he told me. It was almost funny, except for the fact that he was serious.

We spoke well into the night, the three of them telling me stories of prison, of persecution, and of the hope that one day they will be able fight back. They also spoke of their undying loyalty to the United States and of their sadness at being betrayed and forgotten. I sat there in the darkness listening to them, but had little to say to give them hope, but they had much to say to give me none. I walked back to my guesthouse that night alone in the dark.

Between 2001 and 2003, over 2,000 Montagnards fled the Central Highlands for Cambodia, some of them for the second time. One such man was Y Thu, a man I met twice when he was a refugee: once in Mondolkiri in June 2001, and the second time in a UNHCR safe house in Phnom Penh in August 2003. After fleeing to Cambodia following the demonstrations in February 2001, Thu spent nine months in the camp in Mondolkiri. He was then repatriated to Vietnam after the camp closed down in March 2002. Back in his native province of Dak Lak, Thu spent the next eight months under police surveillance, along with the rest of his family. When the police arrested his brother, beat him up, and sent him to prison in December 2002 for allegedly helping people to escape to Cambodia, Thu fled the country again. He walked for one month with two others until they reached the Cambodian town of Snoul. From there, they arranged for a driver to take them to Phnom Penh. When I met him in late August 2003, he was waiting, along with 37 others, to be resettled in the United States. About 1,000 Montagnards had already been resettled in the US since 2001—including Dieu Mien and Y Bion.

About a week after meeting with Thu and the other Monagnards at the UNHCR safe house in Phnom Penh, I met another Montagnard on the other side of the border in the Central Highlands who was trying to leave Vietnam through official channels. His name was Ksor Ricky, a 52-year-old ethnic Jarai introduced to me by Sui Thom. When I met him in his village just south of Boun Me Thuot in September 2003, he had been trying for the past five years, through US government channels, to be granted resettlement in the United States. He was doing this on the basis that he had fought for the US during the war and that he had spent more than four years in re-education camps afterwards. He was frustrated with the process, as he was having trouble with both US and Vietnamese measures.

Vietnamese authorities had confiscated one of his key documents and demanded unaffordable bribes, while he had been waiting for over two years for a reply from his last written request to the US Embassy in Bangkok. Not allowed to practise his Christian religion, forced to live in a New Economic Zone that, as he wrote in his last letter to the US Embassy, 'lacks any facilities such as roads, transportation, and communications systems,' unable to move freely beyond his village, always treated with suspicion and hostility by the authorities because of his wartime allegiance to America, and barely able to eek a living as a coffee farmer, all he wanted was to leave Vietnam and the prison that he called life. When I told him that life in America as an immigrant wouldn't be easy, and asked him what he'd do for work, he replied, 'I don't care. I'll do anything. I'll be a garbage man.'

Once a proud, loyal soldier who fought for America and paid for that service with over four years in prison and a lifetime of suffering, all Ricky wanted now was the chance to be a garbage man in the country he once served. His homeland, as far he as was concerned, had been taken away from him and his people; there was no reason to stay any longer. Summing up his people's plight, he turned to me in sadness and said, 'This forest, this jungle, this land—we lost it all.'

CHAPTER 4

THAILAND:

TERROR IN THE SOUTH

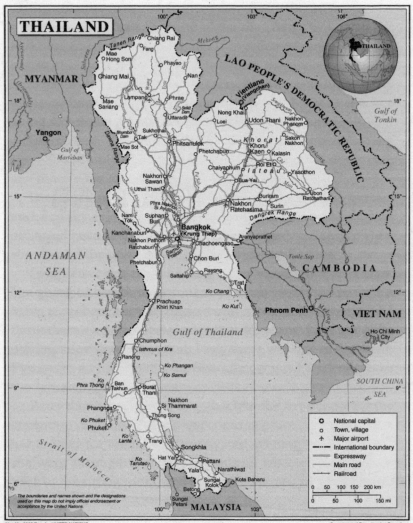

THAILAND

'Don't you have a weapon?' the paramilitary soldier asked me as I was about to accompany his men on a joint patrol with soldiers of the second company of the Thai army's 154th battalion. Before I had time to reply, the commander of the company, Major Somkid Konkaeng, responded to the AK-47-touting irregular, 'I already asked him if he wanted a grenade, but he said no.'

Seemingly surprised and perhaps concerned for my lack of personal protection should we get ambushed or clash with militants on the patrol, the paramilitary turned to me and asked, 'You want an AK?'

Although tempted, I declined. Not so much because of journalistic ethics, but more because I didn't want to carry the extra weight on a potentially arduous foot patrol into the surrounding hills. As for the grenade, I knew I'd be more concerned about accidentally setting it off than concentrating on the actual patrol itself. Besides, when under fire I'm far more comfortable shooting a camera than a weapon.

The morning's mission was to patrol the area for separatist militants, in particular two leaders of a shadowy group known as the Runda Kumpulan Kecil (RKK) believed to be in the area: U Bai Dee La Ramurlee and Makata Hama. According to Major Somkid, in March 2007 U Bai Dee La was responsible for a gruesome attack on a civilian minibus traveling through Somkid's command area on the way to the city of Hat Yai. Militants opened fire on the van and shot all nine passengers at point-blank range. All of the passengers were Buddhist, while only the driver, a Muslim, was spared. Referring to U Bai Dee La, Somkid told me, 'He is the number one man I want to kill.'

I had met Somkid a few days before, in early March 2008, when I arranged through the Thai army's command base in Yala city to be embedded with Thai forces in the area battling an Islamic insurgency. Since January 2004, attacks have occurred on an almost daily basis, making it one of the deadliest Islamic insurgencies in the world. The insurgents, while never making their demands public or claiming responsibility for their attacks, are fighting for an independent Islamic state in the three southernmost provinces of Thailand: Pattani, Yala and Narathiwat, as well as four districts of Songkhla province. The area historically belonged to the Malay Kingdom of Patani until it was formally annexed by Thailand over a century ago. With almost daily violence that includes drive-by shootings, arson attacks and bombings, the three Muslim-majority southernmost provinces of Thailand—one of the world's most visited countries—resembles more of a war zone than a tropical paradise. I guess that's why I'm drawn there.

Immediately after I made my request to be embedded with Thai forces, Colonel Acra Tiproch, the Thai army's spokesman for the southern region, arranged for me to be taken to meet with Lt- Colonel Woradet Detrugsa, commander of the Thai army's 154th battalion based in Yala's Yaha district. After lunch with Acra and a few hundred military, police and government officials in Yala, three men dressed in civilian clothes carrying M-16s picked me up in their truck and drove me to Woradet's camp, located about 30 kilometers west of the city. When I explained to Woradet what I wanted to do, namely to accompany Thai soldiers on an operation or patrol, or at the very least to just spend a few days with an army unit, he immediately arranged for me to be sent to Major Somkid's company based at Ban Pa Tae, also in Yala's Yaha district. I arrived at Somkid's camp, located in a small rubber plantation on the outskirts of the village, and was immediately greeted by the cheerful but tough-looking 33-year-old commander.

Somkid had been stationed in the south for four years, arriving in the region within days after militants raided a Thai army camp in Narathiwat province on 4 January 2004, killing four Buddhist soldiers and making away with over 400 weapons. The incident prompted the government to declare martial law in the area and to deploy an additional 3,000 troops to the south as a new phase of a decades-old insurgency got underway.

'I am here working for my country and for my King,' Somkid told me.

While Thai security forces have been accused of using excessive force and engaging in human rights abuses, which no doubt has fuelled the conflict, Somkid seemed a genuinely sincere man who favored a softer, more conciliatory approach to handling the conflict. Somkid told me his strategy was to use words over weapons—to talk with the local population, befriend them, develop relations with them, gain their trust and work together with them, not against them.

'I came here because I want to make a difference,' he explained to me that afternoon in the camp's open-air meeting area. 'I don't want to use my gun, I just use it to protect my soldiers, my base and me. I prefer to fight with my mouth.'

According to him, his strategy had worked and the situation had been improving over the past year in the nine village areas of Yaha for which his company was responsible. 'Many insurgents have left this area because nobody accepts them,' he told me. But not all—and if Somkid came face to face with U Bai Dee La, the RKK leader believed to be in the area, then he'd choose his M-16 over his mouth.

On the morning of the patrol, I kept right behind him as we set out on foot from the village of Ma Bae in a 12 man team, turning off the main highway onto a small forest track that led us into an expansive rubber plantation. The mission was to cover several kilometers of the jungle plantation and then circle back to the highway near Ma Bae. The mountainous jungle terrain was ideal territory for the insurgents, and our 12 man team was an ideal ambush target for them. For the first time since Cambodia a decade before, I was walking among government forces, not insurgents, and I knew that the latter had the advantage. I was now walking among the prey, and we were patrolling the predator's lands. Perhaps I should have taken a weapon after all.

About an hour into the patrol, as we began to circle back towards the highway, distant shouts could be heard, as if someone in the forest was signaling to another person. Somkid ordered his men to stop. Fearing it was the signal of insurgents, he sent half of the patrol team back in the direction of the calls to check out who was making them. 'If they are armed, shoot them,' he ordered his men. Carefully keeping watch, I waited with Somkid for either his soldiers to return or for the forest to erupt in gunfire. Believing that one of the rubber tree-tappers we had passed earlier was a potential insurgent who was now signaling to his comrades, perhaps to lay an ambush on us, Somkid looked at me in frustration and said, 'I cannot tell the difference between civilians and terrorists in this area.'

Like most Islamic militants, the insurgents of southern Thailand don't wear uniforms, mix in with the local population, and use terrorism as a means to wage their war. They organize themselves in small cells and live among the villagers, making it extremely difficult for the security forces to distinguish them from the ordinary population.

As Colonel Acra explained, 'If the insurgents stayed in the jungle, it would be very easy for us to get rid of them. But they're in the villages and they mix in with the population.'

A platoon commander in Somkid's company, Second-Lieutenant Kosin Soha, echoed Somkid's frustration when he told me, 'My commander told me not to think that everyone is a terrorist, but in reality I can't trust anyone.'

The people signaling to each other in the rubber plantation that morning were not insurgents. As it turned out, they were a young couple communicating to each other that their rubber tapping work was done. In this insurgency, these people were just as likely a target as Somkid's soldiers. Dozens of rubber tappers have been killed in the violence, systematically targeted by militants as part of their campaign of terror, making this mundane line of work one of the deadliest occupations in southern Thailand.

Once Somkid was satisfied with the rubber tappers' story, we continued on towards the highway, arriving in the village of U Beng shortly after. There, Somkid introduced me to Wortae Salae, a 69-year-old ethnic Malay Muslim whose family was torn apart by the insurgency. Of his three sons, one was a militant he hadn't seen since 2004; another was a policeman who was in fear of visiting his family in U Beng because he was sure to be on a militant's hit list; and the last son was already dead—killed by militants. When I asked Wortae what he thought about his militant son, he said that he was brainwashed by a local religious leader, or *ulaman*. The Thai police had already killed the *ulaman*, and when intelligence revealed that the man who took his place was also part of the insurgent network, he was also killed—by Somkid's company.

'*Ulamans* are more dangerous than the terrorists,' Somkid said to me, referring to those who are engaged in the insurgency, 'because they teach people to hate, and they turn people into terrorists.' As for Wortae, he missed his son but hoped he would never return—not because he feared for his son's life, but because he feared his son.

'I'm scared that my son will come back and kill me and our entire family,' he said.

Since 2004, families like those of Wortae have been torn apart by this insurgency that has left the three southernmost provinces of Thailand gripped in fear. It is by no means a new conflict, but rather a new phase of a centuries-old conflict between the Thai state and this predominantly Malay Muslim region that once flourished as the independent Malay Kingdom of Patani. While historical factors may lie at the root of the conflict, the potent mix of ethnic-nationalism and radical Islam in the 21st century has assured its violent ascent.

'Hundreds of years ago, Patani made cannons and sold them to the Japanese,' explained a 26-year-old student activist named Ya over dinner one night to illustrate how powerful his homeland once was. He offered me a local cigarette and said, 'Now we just grow our own tobacco.'

While half-joking, his anecdote summed up the general historical grievances that the ethnic Malay

Muslims of southern Thailand harbor for the Thai state. Speaking their own language, practicing Islam instead of Buddhism, and sharing a distinct Malay culture vastly different from the Thais, they make up about 85 percent of the 1.8 million people who inhabit the Thai provinces of Yala, Narathiwat, Pattani and parts of Songkhla (Patani is the Malay spelling and refers to the former kingdom and region, while Pattani is transliterated from Thai spelling and refers to the province and city). Indeed, their grievances are numerous and legitimate, and began with their long decline from being an independent flourishing kingdom to being unwillingly incorporated into the Thai state; or to paraphrase the words of Ya, from making cannons to growing tobacco.

Established in the 14th century and emerging from the ancient Malay Kingdom of Langkasuka, the Malay Kingdom of Patani was once one of the most prosperous kingdoms in Southeast Asia with its port being one of the busiest and wealthiest in the region. In 1563, nearing the height of its economic and political power, it was able to deploy 200 warships to take advantage of a Burmese attack on Siam (present-day Thailand) to launch an attack of its own against its northern rival. It successfully seized the gate of the royal citadel in Ayutthaya before making a quick retreat and sailing back to Patani. It was the closest the Malays of Patani would ever come to subduing the Thais; from then onwards, they would be at the receiving end of subjugation.

In the late 16th century, with the kingdom's first of four successive queens enthroned, the kingdom entered its golden age, expanded its territory, and became one of the most powerful kingdoms in the region. It was during this period that Patani became renowned for making cannons, producing three of the largest ever cast in the region, and the sale of these cannons (to Japan, for instance), became an important enterprise.

In part due to these superior cannons, Patani was able to hold off four Thai invasions in the first half of the 17th century, driving back their northern rival each time as Siam tried to bring Patani into its expanding empire. While Siam had always claimed rights to Patani and viewed it as a vassal state, with Patani unwillingly a tributary state to Ayutthaya, it wasn't until the late 18th century when Siam's military prowess was finally able to defeat the kingdom and place it under its control. According to one local author of Patani's history, who was writing in the late 1940s under the pseudonym of Ibrahim Syukri, the defeat of 1786 was the first defeat in Patani's history and signified the loss of the kingdom's independence.

Most news reports and analyses of the contemporary conflict in southern Thailand point to Siam's formal annexation of the region in 1902 as the impetus to the current conflict. In reality, however, the region was under Siam's dominance, and at many times control, for much longer. When we look back further in history, the question of who lays the rightful claim on the region becomes even more dubious. As Major Somkid explained, 'The terrorists say Pattani is Muslim land, but before it was Muslim, it was Buddhist, and before Buddhist it was Hindu.'

Indeed, he knew his history well. Interestingly, the Kingdom of Patani was a Buddhist kingdom before it adopted Islam and was declared an Islamic State in 1547. One of the oldest religious relics in the region is a Buddhist idol in a cave outside of Yala that dates back to the eighth century (a place that is still worshipped by Thai Buddhists today), while the ancient Kingdom of Langkasuka, which preceded Patani, was primarily Hindu and was inhabited mainly by Austro-Asiatic speakers who arrived on the Malay Peninsula long before the Malays. One could argue that the Thai state has just as legitimate claims to the region as the Malay Muslims who inhabit it.

Following a series of revolts in the late 18th and early 19th centuries that were successfully quelled by Bangkok (the new capital of Siam), the Patani region was divided into seven small states. Each state had a ruler who was appointed by Bangkok, which effectively dispersed local power in a way that all but dissolved the kingdom. In 1902 Patani was formally annexed by Siam and incorporated into the Thai state—an action that was reinforced in 1909 by an Anglo-Siamese treaty in which the British recognized Siam sovereignty over Patani. In return, Siam gave up its claims to the Malay states of Kelentan, Kedah, Perlis, and Terengganu, which were brought under indirect British rule. As part of this annex, Sharia law was abolished in all cases except those involving marriage and inheritance. Moreover, the local aristocracy was deposed and replaced with Siamese officials who spoke only Thai, had little or no knowledge of local customs, and reported directly to Bangkok. It was a recipe for rebellion.

The first to rebel was Tengku Abdul Kadir, the last sultan, or *raja*, of Pattani (one of the seven states of the former Kingdom of Patani which was broken up by the Thais in the early 19th century). He refused to give his signature to the Siamese envoy in the 1902 annexation and was therefore charged with treason and sent off to prison in Phitsnaulok, north of Bangkok, which sparked protests among his loyal followers. After his release in 1905, he returned to the Patani region where he continued his resistance against Siamese rule. After a failed revolt in 1915, he fled to Kelantan in British Malaya where he continued to exert significant influence on his homeland until his death in 1933. In 1922, he inspired yet another rebellion—the biggest of his career—in which villagers refused to pay land tax in protest against educational reforms announced a year before, which made it compulsory for all Malay Muslim children to attend Thai primary schools for at least four years in order to learn the Thai language. Violent clashes broke out and the rebellion ended in failure as several prominent Muslim leaders were either killed or arrested. However, the rebellion did force Bangkok to revise its educational and taxation policies in the restive south.

Resentment and resistance cooled in the region until the rise to power of the ultra-nationalist Phibun Songkhram in 1938, six years after Siam's absolute monarchy was abolished in favor of constitutional rule.

As part of his Pan-Thai nationalist policy, a series of cultural mandates, or state edicts, were issued, the first of which changed the country's name from Siam to Thailand (i.e. belonging to the Thais). These mandates were issued not only to promote Thai nationalism, but also, in part, to assimilate the country's various ethnic minorities, including the Malay Muslims of the south. Themes of 'Thai-ness' and 'unity' ultimately had a profoundly negative impact on the Malay Muslim way of life. Some of the mandates implemented included the requirement of a modern dress code that forbade traditional dress, the banning of all languages except Thai in government offices, and the establishment of Buddhism as the official state religion. The measures were viewed by many Malay Muslims as aimed directly at them. Of course, the mandates applied to all peoples of Thailand and were in no way directed specifically at the Muslims of the south. While Buddhism was made the official religion of the state, people were still free to practise any other religion, including Islam.

The rise of Thai nationalism in the mid 20th century coincided with the rise of Malay nationalism, not least as a reaction against Bangkok's harsh assimilation policies, which were viewed as being a direct threat against their culture and way of life. One of the leading nationalists to emerge was Haji Sulong, a religious scholar educated in Mecca. As head of the Pattani Provincial Islamic Council and founder of the Patani People's Movement in 1947, he produced a list of seven ethno-religious demands to Bangkok that included self-rule, the implementation of Sharia law, and greater language and cultural rights. The action landed him in prison on charges of treason. Following his arrest, rebellions broke out in the three southernmost provinces, the largest occurring on 26-28 April 1948 in the village of Duson-Nyor in Narathiwat province when about 1,000 villagers clashed with police forces. When the fighting was over after 36 hours, over 400 Muslim villagers were killed along with about 30 police officers.

Haji Sulong was released from prison in 1952 but disappeared two years later along with his eldest son, allegedly killed by Thai police. Dying a martyr, he remains an icon of Malay resistance against the Thai state—and an important reminder of what happens to those who make demands. When I asked Ya, the student activist I met in Pattani in March 2008, why the separatist militants in today's conflict haven't made their demands known, he named Haji Sulong and two other more contemporary figures who met the same fate and said, 'Because anyone who makes demands ends up dead.'

Five years after Haji Sulong's death, the first organized armed resistance group calling for Patani's independence, the Patani National Liberation Front (Barisan Nasional Pembebasan Patani, BNPP) was established. A few years later, another group was established, the Barisan Revolusi Nasional (BRN), with an initial objective to incorporate the southern provinces of Thailand into a pan-Malay state across Southeast Asia, which was soon dropped in favor of an independent republic of Patani. Soon, dozens of armed groups were operating in the region posing a serious security challenge to the Thai state. While many of these groups had no political agenda, being nothing more than criminal gangs, the government was clearly losing its monopoly over force in the area. The region was turning into a place of lawlessness, which has never fully been tamed. Indeed, since then, political violence has coincided with a mixture of criminal activity, blurring the lines between conflict and crime. One of the foremost experts on the contemporary conflict in southern Thailand, Dr Srisompob Jitpiromsri, a political science lecturer at Pattani's Prince of Songkhla University, told me that he estimates that 20 percent of the current violence is related to criminal activity, while 70 percent is the work of insurgents. The other ten percent, he said, was caused by security forces, usually in the form of extrajudicial killings of terrorist suspects.

The largest and most effective armed separatist group to emerge in southern Thailand in the 1970s was the Patani United Liberated Organization (PULO), established in 1968 with the goal of creating an independent Islamic state. Most of PULO's leaders were based in Mecca, and the group even had a training camp in Syria. At the height of separatist activity during this period, from the mid 1970s to the early 1980s, PULO was responsible for the majority of insurgent attacks in southern Thailand. It claimed its strength at 20,000 men, although most reliable estimates put their strength at not even a thousand.

The insurgency died down in the 1980s due to an overhaul of the government's strategy in handling the situation under the leadership of General Prem Tinsulanonda who held power from 1980 to 1988. Some of the key policies implemented to quell the conflict included the establishment of more responsive administrative and security bodies in the south, the channeling of development funds into the area, increasing Malay-Muslim participation in the government, and providing a blanket amnesty for separatists who laid down their weapons. By the end of the decade, the Thai government estimated that there were only 300 to 500 insurgents left, and by the end of the 1990s, only 150 to 200.

Although the insurgency had been allayed, it was far from dead. Instead, the conflict mutated into a more radical form as splinter groups and newcomers began to emerge with more pronounced Islamist agendas. Both PULO and BRN fissured, with BRN having three distinct factions as early as 1984: BRN-Congress, BRN-Coordinate and BRN-Ulama. While pursuing a more long-term political strategy, BRN-Coordinate (BRN-C) infiltrated Islamic schools (*pondoks*) where they built up a strong and loyal support base. They would eventually emerge two decades later as the largest, best organized and most lethal militant group in the south, spearheading the renewed insurgency in 2004. Likewise, PULO began to split in the 1980s but didn't officially separate until 1995 with the formation of New PULO. This was a breakaway group that advocated a sustained, low-level insurgency with the lesser aim of autonomy rather than independence. Also in 1995 was the founding of the Patani Islamic Mujahidin Movement (GMIP) by a Malay Muslim veteran of the Afghan-Soviet war. GMIP's goal was to create an Islamic state in southernmost Thailand but it was generally dismissed by Thai authorities as merely a criminal gang due to their involvement in kidnappings and extortion. Its leaders, however, apparently never lost their zeal for Islamic fundamentalism, nor did they forget the allegiances that were formed during their time in Afghanistan. In late 2001, the group reportedly distributed leaflets in Yala calling for jihad and for support to Osama Bin Laden.

On Christmas Eve that same year, militants attacked five police posts in the provinces of Pattani, Yala, and Narathiwat, killing five police officers and a village defence volunteer. Not only was it the biggest attack launched in years, but it was also the first time in the history of armed separatism in southernmost Thailand that insurgents had launched a coordinated attack across the three provinces, a clear indication that they were well organized and had changed their tactics. According to the Thai Ministry of Interior, a total of 50 people were killed in southern Thailand that year in insurgency-related incidents. That number rose to 75 in the year 2002; 119 in 2003 and then skyrocketed to over 1,000 in 2004. The vast majority of those who died were civilians. Terror had come to Thailand.

The new phase of the insurgency began on 4 January 2004 when around 100 militants launched a pre-dawn raid on the Ratchanakarin camp of the Thai army's 4th Engineering Battalion in Narathiwat's Joh Airong district. The raiders made away with over 400 weapons including assault rifles, machine guns, pistols and rocket-propelled grenade launchers. They killed four Buddhist soldiers in the process but spared the Muslim guards looking after the arsenal. This raid coincided with arson attacks on 20 schools and three police posts across Narathiwat province. The government of Thaksin Shinawatra, elected in 2001, responded by declaring martial law in eight districts of the south, later extended to include all of the three provinces of Narathiwat, Yala and Pattani, set an unrealistic deadline of seven days for authorities to arrest the perpetrators, and deployed an additional 3,000 troops to the southern region of the country.

In February 2004, authorities arrested several suspects, at least five of whom confessed to being involved in the raid, although it was later revealed that their confessions were made under police torture. One of those arrested was 52-year-old Do Loe Seng Ma Su, the village headman of Ban Ta Lo Wae in Yala's Yaha district. I met and interviewed him at his village in March 2008 where he was back carrying out his duties as chief of the village. He was a former PULO insurgent who joined the group in 1977 and served for 14 years until accepting amnesty and surrendering to the government in 1991. Two years later he was elected the village chief, or *phu yai*, of Ban Ta Lo Wae. Police had arrested him in Yala in February 2004, accusing him of still supporting PULO and taking part in the 4 January raid, even though the raid had not been attributed to PULO. He vehemently denied the accusation, telling me he was at his home when the attack took place. When I asked him why he thought he was arrested, he simply replied, 'Politics.'

He was taken to Bangkok where he spent the next 21 months in prison until he was released, according to him, on the recommendation of a lieutenant-general in the Thai army. He returned to his village where he resumed his duties as *phu yai*, which, on three occasions, has nearly cost him his life. The first two times were in March 2007, when, because of his allegiance to the government, militants launched two assassination attempts on him. After escaping unharmed in the first attempt, militants shot him in the face on the second. He lost an eye, but survived. Eight months later in November, he was the target of a third assassination attempt when militants placed a bomb on the road in his village and waited for his vehicle to pass by to detonate it. Following a tip-off, soldiers of Major Somkid's company arrived at the scene before the attack took place. They battled the nine militants in a gunfight that left one of the assailants dead while the others fled. The bomb was defused and the village headman escaped again with his life.

'They want to kill me because I work for the government,' he told me. When I asked him how much his salary was, thinking perhaps the money was worth risking his life for, he replied, 'I don't get one.'

When the renewed insurgency began in 2004, the government wanted him in prison. Now, the militants want him dead. After talking with him, I remembered the words of a Malay Muslim student leader named Cha who I had interviewed a few days before. As an activist for human rights and justice in the south, he was angered by the actions of the Thai state, and was therefore treading on dangerous ground. Two of his friends had already been arrested and allegedly tortured by the security forces for their purported involvement in the insurgency, while another was shot dead in a protest in October 2004. 'If you fight, you will die,' Cha told me. 'If you don't fight, you will also die.' Those words were especially apt for the village headman of Ban Ta Lo Wae.

In addition to the 4 January arms raid, two other major incidents occurred in 2004 that had profound effects on the situation in southern Thailand. The first occurred on 28 April when over 100 militants, many of them armed with just machetes, launched simultaneous pre-dawn attacks on police bases and checkpoints in several districts of Yala, Pattani and Songkhla provinces. By mid afternoon, almost all of them were dead, including 31 who were holed up in the historic Krue-Se mosque in Pattani. The attackers belonged to a group known as *Hikmat Allah Abadan* (Brotherhood of the Eternal Judgement of God) led by Ustadz Soh, a radical Muslim who claimed to have supernatural powers. While he himself didn't take part in the attack (perhaps because he wasn't as confident in his godlike powers as he had led some to believe), many of the assailants were given 'sacred water' to make them invisible. Some of them even sprinkled 'magical sand' on roads to prevent military vehicles from reaching Krue-Se. Needless to say, the magic didn't work.

After an eight-hour stand-off at the mosque, during which two members of the security forces were shot dead by the militants inside, Special Forces troops successfully stormed the mosque and shot dead all the assailants inside, many at point-blank range. Human rights organizations immediately condemned the Thai army for excessive use of force, even though the assailants were armed, refused offers to surrender, and killed two soldiers during the stand-off. The event has been repeatedly cited as one of the prime examples of the Thai government's mishandling of the conflict and a key episode that has fuelled resentment among the local population because of the military's hard-line tactics. While the Thai army was criticized by local and international human rights groups, including the United Nations High Commission for Human Rights, not one human rights group condemned the assailants for launching a day of jihad against the Thai state, or for using excessive force by killing five members of the security forces that day. As Major Somkid told me almost four years after the event: 'If I was in command at Krue-Se that day, I would have done the same.'

The third pivotal event to occur in 2004 after the arms raid and Krue-Se was the quelling of a protest in Tak Bai, Narathiwat on 25 October. Villagers had gathered around a police station to protest the arrest of six Muslim men who were village defense volunteers being detained for giving their state-issued weapons to militants. The villagers believed they had been wrongly arrested on the grounds that they did not willingly give their weapons to the militants but were forced to do so. Before long, the crowd swelled to over 1,500 people, some of whom tried to break through a police barrier to enter the station. While initially the security forces used tear gas and water cannons to try and disperse the crowd, they soon resorted to firing their weapons; most were only warning shots, but not all. When the chaos subsided, some 1,300 men and boys were loaded into army trucks (women and children were allowed to leave the area) and driven to an army camp in Pattani about 150 kilometers away. Along the way, 78 of them perished, suffocating to death in the trucks. This time, it was more than just an excessive use of force.

The incidents at Krue-Se and Tak Bai in 2004 have come to symbolize the Thai government's heavy-handed approach to dealing with the insurgency. They have also exemplified the willingness of the security forces to use excessive force and to do so with impunity. Without doubt, such heavy-handed tactics that have been embodied in these two events have fueled anger and resentment among the local population and have been detrimental to the government's counter-insurgency campaign. Indeed, such heavy-handed tactics and the abuse of human rights perpetrated by the security forces, which has included extrajudicial killings, arbitrary arrests, forced disappearances and torture, have come to be a hallmark of the conflict in southern Thailand. Hearts and minds have been anything but won.

On the morning of 27 January 2008, about 30 plain-clothes military agents raided a dormitory of Yala's Rajabhat University and arrested five students and two of their friends. Accused of being insurgents, the group was taken to a nearby military camp of Task Force 11 and then transferred to Inkayuthboriharn army camp in Pattani where they were detained and interrogated for nine days. Two of those who were arrested were Isma-ae Teh and Ameesee Manak. Both were aged 22 and in their third year of studies. I met them a little over a month after their ordeal.

In an empty cafeteria at Prince of Songkhla University in Pattani, Isma-ae got on his hands and knees while Ameesee grabbed his neck and pretended to choke him. He then shouted at him to try and make him confess to being an insurgent. They were demonstrating to me just one of the ways they were tortured while in army custody during those nine terrifying days. Besides being choked, they said they were kicked, punched, and beaten with guns, tire spokes and pieces of wood wrapped in cloth.

They told me they were innocent and, despite being tortured, they refused to confess to being insurgents. When I asked them why they thought they were arrested, they said that they had been involved in student activities such as the organization of human rights and legal training seminars. The last seminar had ended only a week before their arrest.

'The government sees us as militants, as criminals, but we are doing good things,' Isma-ae told me. 'If the government arrests us and sees us as militants, it means the government sees all the people as militants.'

Without sufficient evidence of being linked to the insurgency, the group was released after nine days. With martial law in effect in southernmost Thailand, suspects can be held for seven days without charge, after which they can be held for another 30 days under an Emergency Decree put in place in July 2005 under the government of Thaksin Shinawatra. Suspects are also prohibited from having family and lawyer visits during the first 72 hours of their detention. From July 2005 to January 2008, more than 3,300 people were detained at the Inkayuthboriharn army camp in Pattani where Isma-ae and Ameesee were held (the army's main interrogation center in the south), with the vast majority of those being released due to insufficient evidence to bring their cases to trial.

These mass arrests have undoubtedly further alienated the Malay Muslim population of the south, especially youths, who have often been the ones detained. However, according to the Thai army, these arrests have also contributed to a significant decrease in violence. This indicates that such sweeping arrests are anything but arbitrary and are indeed disrupting the insurgents' networks and operational capabilities. Army commanders have repeatedly told me that, while the majority of those arrested are eventually released, they believe that this is not because they are innocent, but rather because there is not enough evidence to bring their case to trial, let alone convict them.

While Isma-ae and Ameesee had their gripes with the Thai state before their arrest, now they were outraged.

'[The authorities] treat us like animals, like people who don't have brains and people who can't think,' Isma-ae told me. Though both Isma-ae and Ameesee denied any links to the insurgents, they were clearly sympathetic to their cause. As was Ya, the student activist who was also present that afternoon. In May 2007, he founded the Student's Network for Protecting the People, a group that documents human rights abuses allegedly committed by the authorities.

'The government must give justice to the people,' he told me, citing the issues of justice and human rights as key elements that have fueled the conflict and have caused people to join the insurgents. 'The people here don't trust the justice system of the state,' Ya added.

When I asked if he would consider joining the militants, he replied, 'I would have to see the real objective of their struggle. If their objective is to return freedom to the people, I would join.'

Consumed by anger at the Thai state, and being highly nationalistic, Ya was clearly a candidate for militancy. 'I'm not a Thai person,' he told me, 'my DNA is not Thai. But the Thai government wants me to be Thai. My ID card says my nationality is Thai, but I'm not Thai. I'm Melayu,' he said, using the Malay language name for a Malay person.

The next day, I accompanied Ya, Isma-ae and Ameesee to two villages in Pattani and Yala to collect information on two recent shootings allegedly committed by government paramilitary forces. Both villages were considered 'red zones', villages loosely designated by the authorities as insurgent hotbeds. A year after the renewed insurgency began in January 2004, there were some 215 such villages; by March 2008, there were about 320.

The first village we went to was Ban Krulong in Pattani's Panarae district, a small Muslim village surrounded by four Buddhist villages. When we arrived, over a dozen villagers gathered to see us and recounted to us the story of a recent shooting, which they believed was carried out by paramilitary forces. According to the villagers, on the evening of 22 February 2008, two teenage boys on a motorbike were stopped at an intersection waiting for a truck to pass by on the main road. But instead of passing, the truck stopped and a man dressed in black sitting in the back of the pick-up opened fire on the boys with his pistol, killing the 15-year-old driver of the motorbike and injuring a 16-year-old boy who was walking behind the motorbike. As the truck sped off, another villager followed it, claiming that it drove into a nearby army camp. When that villager reported what had happened to the police, he was dismissed as a liar. According to the villagers, the police investigation into the incident took 30 minutes and the case was closed after compensation of 10,000 Baht (about US$320) was given to the family of the teenager that was killed, and 7,500 Baht was given to the boy that was wounded.

'There is no justice here,' one villager told me, 'we cannot trust the justice system; it cannot help us.'

The people of Ban Krulong lived in fear—and it wasn't the militants they were scared of. Ethnic tension was so high in the area that they claimed they were too intimidated to leave their village. Referring to their relationships with the four Buddhist villages that surrounded Ban Krulong, one of the villagers explained to me, 'Before, we could communicate with each other, we were friends, but since 2004 we cannot even pass their villages, we will be threatened—the Buddhist villagers are armed … they threaten us by showing us their weapons.'

'We are all afraid,' another villager told me. 'Even just to go to the mosque, which is a normal thing to do, we fear. We don't know if we will get shot, and if we do who will help us. We go to work with fear, but we must go to work, if not, how can we survive?'

Another villager, an elderly man, told me how he was hit in the face by a beer bottle someone had thrown from a passing vehicle into the village's mosque where he had been praying. He was sure the culprit was a Buddhist from a neighboring village.

'In the eyes of the government,' another villager told me, 'we are bad people.' Another villager asked, 'if we wear Muslim dress, if we go to a mosque, does that make us militants?' All of the villagers I spoke to refused to give their names for security concerns—all except Marken Ngok, the 16-year-old boy who was wounded in the shooting, and his two friends that were present when the incident took place, 15-year-old Ricky Darama and 11-year-old Kamaro Lateh, both of whom escaped unharmed. When I asked them why they thought government paramilitaries wanted to kill them, they said they had no idea why.

The government has relied extensively on paramilitary forces to combat the insurgency in the south, with several different groups working alongside and often in conjunction with regular army and police units. The largest is the Village Defense Volunteers (Chor Ror Bor), which constitutes the main form of security in most villages, and numbers almost 50,000. A typical village in the south has a force of 30 Chor Ror

Bor and receives a monthly budget of 20,000 Baht for the entire force. Their main duties are to guard the village's checkpoint and provide security for the headman and other leaders, and also for the schools, teachers and government infrastructure. After the Chor Ror Bor, the next biggest paramilitary force in the south is the 'Ranger' force (Thahan Phran), which by the end of 2008 numbered about 9,000. Their main duties include manning checkpoints and conducting foot patrols, often through the jungle or on small back roads. They have also been known to conduct assassinations. The villagers of Ban Krulong believed it was the Thahan Phran that conducted the shooting of the boys on 22 February 2008. However, militants have also been known to carry out attacks dressed in black like the Thahan Phran in order to boost anti-government sentiment.

In addition to the Chor Ror Bor and the Thahan Phran, there is the Village Defense Corps (Or Sor), as well as several other village volunteer forces, and an unknown number of sectarian militias. Paramilitary forces are used extensively because they cost little to deploy and have a profound knowledge of the local area. But they are also ill-equipped, poorly trained, and often lack in discipline. Paramilitaries have also been involved in numerous controversial incidents which have no doubt contributed significantly to the state's negative reputation among the Malay Muslim population. However, for the Buddhist minority in the south who feel under attack, paramilitaries are viewed in a much more positive light—as protectors and defenders against the militants who want to drive them out.

The second village we went to after Ban Krulong that day was Bujoh Bumang in Yala's Ramen district, one of the most violent districts in the south. When we arrived, about 40 women were waiting for us in a house with dried blood splattered on the floor and numerous bullet holes. The women had come from nine different villages nearby—all to voice their grievances against the Thai authorities, and in particular against the latest incident that took place in this house. No men were present because they were too afraid to leave their villages.

According to the women, on the evening of 7 March 2008, seven or eight men dressed in black surrounded the house and then broke in. A woman was sleeping on the floor near the door and her husband was chopping food with a knife nearby. The husband's 100-year-old mother, who was suffering from Alzheimer's, was in a separate room in the back. The intruders immediately opened fire with AK-47 assault rifles and M-16s. When they stopped shooting, there was half a kilogram of shell casings on the floor and two bodies lying in pools of blood. According to the women, the perpetrators were Thahan Phran. While there was no way to confirm this, what didn't need confirmation was the fact that the people here, as in Ban Krulong, lived in fear of the Thai authorities.

'We don't want Thai soldiers here,' one of the women told me. 'Before, we lived happily without them.' Over the next hour or so, the women relentlessly told me of their grievances, as if these complaints had been bottled up for so long and now they were finally able to vent them.

'We need justice!' snapped one. 'We feel frustrated,' added another. 'We are so desperate. If we speak, there is no one to help us. If we speak, we put ourselves more at risk. So right now we can only be silent.'

Like the villagers of Ban Krulong, the women here felt that the Thai state could not provide them with justice. They had no trust in the justice system of the state and no means of safeguarding their own protection. They also felt that the Thai state was infringing on their traditional way of life, especially with respect to the state's prohibition on the teaching of their traditional Yawi language in schools (a dialect of Malay). 'This is our home,' one woman told me, 'this is our land. But we cannot choose our own destiny.'

Language, along with education, has long been a source of contention between the Thai state and the Malay Muslims of southern Thailand. As language is an important marker of identity, attempts by Thai authorities dating back decades to impose the use of the Thai language upon them—both in schools and as the working language of the region—have been viewed as a means of forced assimilation by the Thai state, an attack on their culture and way of life, and have always been met with resistance. While the Yawi language is taught in the numerous religious schools in the area, the Thai language remains the medium of instruction in state schools, which, according to law, all children must attend for seven years (although this is rarely enforced).

Attempts also to regulate and control traditional Islamic schools (*pondoks*), which began in the 1950s, intensified in the early 1960s and again after the renewed insurgency began in 2004, have also stirred resentment as *pondoks* are viewed by the local populace as the primary institution by which their religion and culture are preserved and transmitted. Any attempt by the Thai state to control or regulate them is viewed as a direct attack on the Muslim culture, religion and way of life.

However, such institutions, especially in recent years, have become fertile breeding grounds of militants. Furthermore, regulation is needed to ensure the quality of education that is being taught at such institutions. 'The problem with traditional Islamic schools is that we don't know what they teach,' explained an educational trainer at the Pattani Educational College —an articulate and highly educated Buddhist woman who has lived most of her life in the south.

'If they teach the components, that's fine, but if they don't, it's dangerous.' She told me how she was responsible for training teachers, many of them teachers of Islamic kindergartens, or *tidikas*, and how many of them were ridiculously underqualified. 'Some haven't even finished high school and they are teaching at *tidikas*,' she told me. 'Some teachers are 15 years old. This is inappropriate.'

Generalizing all *tidika* teachers, she told me, 'They like to teach, but they don't have anything to teach.'

Nevertheless, traditional Islamic schools are regarded as the storehouses of Malay Muslim culture. Ya was particularly furious at the government's strict control of such institutions, and when I pointed out to him that they have been proven to be recruitment places of militants, he replied, 'I don't know if they're recruitment places or not, but these schools are a center of culture for the Melayu people. If there is recruitment, it's because the government hasn't let us keep our identity.'

Practically every Malay Muslim and sympathetic and/or well-informed Thai person I have spoken to during my times in southern Thailand cited the issues of justice and human rights as being at the forefront of the many problems there. As one student activist told me, Apisak Sukkasem, a Thai Buddhist who was highly sympathetic to the plight of the Malay Muslims and highly critical of the government's hard-line approach in dealing with the conflict, 'People here won't want to fight if they have justice and human rights.'

While justice and human rights may be at the forefront of the current problems, they are by no means at the root of the current conflict; rather, I believe them to be casualties of it. In my view, the conflict in southern Thailand is about identity; or, according to Samuel Huntington's famously entitled classic of political science, *The Clash of Civilizations*, it is about exactly this—a clash of civilizations—between the Malay Muslims and the Thai Buddhist state. And when Islamic fundamentalism is involved, such a clash is sure to be bloody and defined by terror.

I was having dinner with Ya, Isma-ae, Ameesee and a few other student activists along the Pattani River when we heard the sound of a distant explosion. About ten minutes before, Ya was telling me how the city of Pattani was one of the most peaceful places in the violence-plagued south of Thailand. This night was an exception. When I returned to my hotel about an hour after we heard the explosion, dozens of police and military officials were gathered around the front entrance, securing the area, and combing through the carnage of a powerful bomb blast. In one of the biggest and boldest bomb attacks ever launched in southern Thailand, militants drove a car armed with three fire extinguishers filled with 10 kilograms of explosives each, parked the car in front of the hotel's terrace restaurant where it could create maximum damage, left the scene, and detonated it. The Muslim driver of the hotel's owner was instantly killed, while the restaurant's Muslim chef, who was walking back to the restaurant after buying something at a nearby store, died later in hospital. In addition, over a dozen more people were injured, including the owner of the hotel, who was also a newly appointed senator. The blast tore up a row of vehicles parked nearby and shattered all the windows on the front of the eight-floor hotel, including mine, room 507.

I began taking pictures of the carnage as soon as I arrived. The scene was a dismal array of blown-up cars, shattered glass, pieces of metal, car parts, blood, and even a pair of sandals. I asked a policeman if anyone died and how many were injured. He answered that one person had been killed and 13 injured, after which he started questioning me. 'Is this your car?' he asked, referring to one that was hit with shrapnel from the blast.

'No,' I replied.

'Where were you when the blast occurred?' the cop asked, making me a bit uncomfortable.

'I was eating dinner.'

'Where were you eating dinner?'

'I don't know, near the river.'

'Who were you eating dinner with?'

'Some friends.'

'Did they take you there?'

I suddenly realized I should now shut up as I didn't want to say I was eating with several Malay Muslim student activists, two of whom were detained a little over a month ago on suspicion of being linked to the insurgency. Just then, another policeman came up to us and again asked me if this was my car. 'No,' I replied, and quietly walked away and resumed taking pictures.

Around midnight, I went to the reception to ask if I could still stay the night. Almost everyone in the hotel had already checked-out, but there was no way in hell that I was going to let terrorists make me check out of my favorite hotel in Thailand. Besides, it was now probably the safest place in the south. Without a problem, the receptionist gave me my key and I went to my room. As I expected, I found the window shattered and glass scattered all over, mainly on the two nice chairs by the window with my laundry drying over them. I went back downstairs to the receptionist and asked to change rooms, to which they happily gave me the key to room 510 across the hall. When I checked out over a week later, they didn't charge me for that night. The CS Pattani hotel remains, without a doubt, my favorite hotel in Thailand.

Like always, no one claimed responsibility for the attack and, while local speculation was rife that it was a personal hit on the owner, Thai senator Anusart Suwanmongkol, and not the work of separatist militants, a second car with identical bombs blew up prematurely on the same afternoon in Yala, killing the driver as he was delivering it, which indicated it was meant to be a coordinated attack and was thus the work of militants. Three months later, in June 2008, I interviewed a former insurgent who said he was part of a six-man bomb team that was in charge of carrying out the Yala bombing that day, confirming it was an orchestrated attack by insurgents. He said the intended target in Yala was the Parkview Hotel, one of Yala's main hotels. The man I interviewed was captured by the security forces on 2 May and was now working as a government spy. For security reasons, he didn't want me to publish his name. Coincidently, he also revealed to me that the seven people arrested at Yala's Rajabhat University on 27 January 2008—who included Isma-ae Teh and Ameesee Manak—were indeed part of an insurgent cell. Lieutenant-Colonel Tanud, commander of the Thai army's 503rd battalion (also known as Yala 11), who was part of the raiding team on 27 January, also told me Isma-ae and Ameesee were part of an insurgent cell but there was not enough evidence to bring them to trial because they only provided logistical support to the insurgency. 'I confirm they are RKK,' he told me.

The bombing of the CS Pattani Hotel on 15 March was not only significant because of the size and sophistication of the attack, but also because of its location. The hotel had long been considered a 'neutral ground' because it was a venue for conferences, meetings and debates among government officials, Muslim clerics, human rights activists and local politicians. It was literally one of the only safe havens in the region; attacking it was a clear message by the militants that nowhere in the south was safe. According to Dr Srisompob Jitpiromsri, the political science lecturer at Prince of Songkhla University (PSU) in Pattani, who I interviewed a few days after the attack, the bombing was also a message to moderates and to the civic movement which had been gaining strength recently. 'The CS hotel is a kind of open space,' he explained to me from his office in the political science department of PSU, 'a place where civic organizations, local leaders and people who are not committed to either side have activities ... the attack was a warning sign to the civic movement and moderates that they cannot create their own games in this conflict.'

He said it also reinforced the message that the insurgents don't want to talk and they don't want dialogue. 'They just want collateral damage,' he said. With the CS hotel attacked, he was now concerned that his university may be another target. After all, he said, there were insurgent cells active at the university, although he believed they were just political units. 'Some are my students,' he said.

Despite the terror and carnage that the militants have unleashed upon southern Thailand, and the actions that the Thai government and the security forces have taken to counter the insurgency, relatively little is known about the insurgents and their organizations. Indeed, their strategy of never claiming responsibility for attacks, never publicly stating their demands, and masking their activities with a high level of secrecy seems to have worked. However, the security forces appear to be making significant gains in unmasking the face of their enemy.

There is little doubt that the group spearheading the insurgency is BRN-Coordinate (BRN-C), the strongest faction of the Barisan Revolusi Nasional (BRN) to emerge following the group's fissure in the 1980s. The group is a grass-roots organization which operates primarily at the village level. Militancy is just one component of what appears to be a fairly sophisticated organizational framework that has enabled the mobilization of a significant amount of the population throughout southernmost Thailand. Besides armed units, the group has a youth wing known as *Pemuda*, village-based committees, and an expansive system of underground networks that focus on activities such as religious indoctrination, social mobilization, and providing logistical and financial support for militants to carry out their campaigns.

The military wing of BRN-C is the RKK (the abbreviation for the Indonesian term for 'small patrol group'). RKK members are trained in weapon handling, hand-to-hand combat, bomb making, sharp-shooting, and ambush tactics. Their weapons include M-16s,

AK-47s, 9mm and 11mm pistols, shotguns, hand grenades, IEDs (improvised explosive devices), and machetes. Most of RKK's activities revolve around four main tactics: assassinations, bomb attacks, arson and ambushes on security forces. Many ambushes involve support from members of *Pemuda*, who generally help by blocking roads with trees or nails in order to cut off escape routes and stall government reinforcements from entering the area.

Like its political umbrella, the RKK operates in small cells of usually between six and eight people. It appears that the various cells have a large degree of independence, with some cells more brutal than others. However, the insurgents have shown on numerous occasions their ability to launch coordinated attacks throughout the three southernmost provinces, indicating that there is a level of hierarchy, control and communication among the cells and between the cells and leaders.

While the Thai military believes that there is a military structure with command and control procedures, another theory suggests that the insurgents are not well organized and that the leaders do not have full control over the insurgency. According to Dr Srisompob, military intelligence has not been able to penetrate the top leadership of BRN-C and other groups because there is nothing there to penetrate. 'Army intelligence so far cannot penetrate to the top of the [various] organizations. They can never do it because they don't have it. They work independently. They are very clever.' He estimates that there are between 3,000 and 5,000 insurgents, and that roughly ten percent of the region's 1.2 million Malay Muslims support their cause.

To date, the insurgents of southern Thailand have refrained from using suicide attacks, but the terror tactics they do employ are just as heinous. While security forces are targeted, so too is anyone associated with the government (from civil servants to primary school teachers), the Buddhist minority (from monks to food vendors) and Muslim collaborators. Killings are often carried out in a highly brutal fashion such as burnings and beheadings. The insurgents also launch indiscriminate attacks as part of their campaign of terror, usually in the form of bombings at public places.

While it is highly likely that BRN-C's networks extend beyond the far south of Thailand into other areas of the country, including Bangkok, the group appears content to limit their militant activities to the three southernmost provinces and parts of Songkhla, i.e. the lands that they view as rightfully theirs. For now, their terror has been contained.

In addition to BRN-C/RKK, there are two other main separatist militant groups operating in the south: New Pulo and GMIP, although neither have anywhere near the strength and capacity of BRN-C/RKK. Surprisingly, no group, including BRN-C, has tried to undermine any of the others in order to build up its own power base and take full control of the insurgency; instead the groups appear content to merge their identities into what can be characterized as a broad separatist front that works together to achieve the ultimate goal of establishing an independent

Islamic state for Patani. In this way, they have further frustrated and limited the capabilities of the security forces to counter the insurgency.

At the time of writing, there has been no concrete evidence linking any foreign groups such as Al-Qaeda to the violence, while so far the area and the conflict has not attracted foreign jihad fighters. However, members of Jemaah Islamiyah (JI), an Indonesian-based terrorist organization with ties to Al-Qaeda, appear to be involved in some training activities in the area while many of the insurgents have received training in Indonesia and other Muslim countries. While the conflict remains first and foremost a separatist struggle, there is always the risk of it being hijacked by foreign elements looking for new and fertile ground on which to wage their global jihad. Furthermore, while at the time of writing the conflict remains contained and the likelihood of the militants succeeding in their separatist campaign is almost negligible, the volatile situation has the potential to turn into a bloody ethnic and communal conflict between Malay Muslims and Thai Buddhists that would pit communities, villages and neighbors against each other.

In all likelihood, the current struggle will not be ending any time soon, although the security forces appear more optimistic. Colonel Acra Tiproch, the Thai army's spokesman for the southern region, told me in March 2008 that he believed the majority of the violence would be quelled in about a year. The student activists I met were much less optimistic.

'The government took 30 years to defeat the communists,' Apisak told me, referring to the country's communist insurgency that lasted from the 1960s until the 1980s. 'But it will take a thousand years to defeat the insurgents here, or until every Melayu person is killed.'

MORE NON-FICTION FROM MAVERICK HOUSE

SECRET GENOCIDE

The Karen of Burma

By DANIEL PEDERSEN

It is almost 60 years since the Karen took up arms against the Burmese dictatorship to fight for an independent homeland, but theirs is a nationalist struggle that shows no sign of exhaustion.

Secret Genocide is a scholarly book on the plight of the Karen of Burma. Author Daniel Pedersen writes about the secret genocide of the Karen people at the hands of the Burmese junta, who use murder, rape, forced labour and torture to quell their enemies. Decades after the Karen took up arms against Rangoon; there is no telling when— or if—their struggle for a secure homeland will be finally accomplished.

To order this book go to www.maverickhouse.com

WELCOME TO HELL

One Man's Fight for Life inside the 'Bangkok Hilton'

By COLIN MARTIN

Written from his cell and smuggled out page by page, Colin Martin's autobiography chronicles an innocent man's struggle to survive inside one of the world's most dangerous prisons.

After being swindled out of a fortune, Martin was let down by the hopelessly corrupt Thai police. Forced to rely upon his own resources, he tracked down the man who conned him and, drawn into a fight, accidentally stabbed and killed the man's bodyguard.

Martin was arrested, denied a fair trial, convicted of murder and thrown into prison—where he remained for eight years. Honest and often disturbing, *Welcome to Hell* is the remarkable story of how Martin was denied justice again and again.

In his extraordinary account, he describes the swindle, his arrest and vicious torture by police, the unfair trial, and the eight years of brutality and squalor he was forced to endure.

To order this book go to www.maverickhouse.com

NIGHTMARE IN LAOS

By KAY DANES

Hours after her husband Kerry was kidnapped by the Communist Laos government, Kay Danes tried to flee to Thailand with her two youngest children, only to be intercepted at the border.

Torn away from them and sent to an undisclosed location, it was then that the nightmare really began. Forced to endure 10 months of outrageous injustice and corruption, she and her husband fought for their freedom from behind the filth and squalor of one of Laos' secret gulags.

Battling against a corrupt regime, she came to realise that there were many people worse off held captive in Laos—people without a voice, or any hope of freedom. Kay had to draw from the strength and spirit of those around her in order to survive this hidden hell, while the world media and Australian government tried desperately to have her and Kerry freed before it was too late and all hope was lost.

For Kay, the sorrow and pain she saw people suffer at the hands of the regime in Laos, where human rights are non-existent, will stay with her forever, and she vowed to tell the world what she has seen. This is her remarkable story.

To order this book go to www.maverickhouse.com